For the Love of God

Prayer Handbook 1996

Prayers by

Michael and Susan Durber

other material
written and selected by

Janet Wootton (Editor).

Introduction

This year's Prayer Handbook has been written by the Revds
Michael and Susan Durber. They worked lovingly and
humorously together, and, at the end, were hard put to it
themselves to remember who had written which prayers.

The theme, *For the Love of God* was their choice, arising from
the Lectionary which focuses in this year on John's gospel.
Running through this gospel is a characteristic theme of love:
God's love for the world, Jesus' love for the disciples and their
love for each other. Where the searchlight of this love encounters
people who are happier in the darkness, other emotions are
kindled: murderous hate, lethal indifference, fear.

Through the prayers, then, the drama of the life of Jesus unfolds,
touching our lives at every point. The prayers are supported by
editor's pages which are different from those of previous years.
The most obvious change is the order. The editor's pages precede
the prayers, and are intended as a preparation for them.

There are several kinds of preparation. Some of the pages are
simply commentary on the text, often linking themes through
John's gospel, or with other scriptural writers, while others take
stories from people's lives. Sometimes there are exercises which
can be done by an individual or group. There are also two songs,
the music for which can be found after Christmas 1 and before the
indexes. As well as words, there are illustrations by Craig Russell.
These are also intended to aid reflection, and groups or individuals
may like to spend some time looking carefully at them, allowing
the images to engage with the words around them.

We hope that the interaction between the editor's pages and the
writers' prayers will enrich the use of the book in private prayer,
as individuals are encouraged to set the prayer in the context of an
act of reflection or worship. Those who use the book in groups or
in public worship should also find that there is material which aids
the development of group experience, which will find expression in
the words of the prayers.

Towards the end of the book, the Lectionary moves on to a new year, beginning with the 9th Sunday before Christmas, and the gospel of Matthew is introduced. We have given the proper Lectionary readings in the heading of the page, but the prayers continue to refer to John's gospel, and to the passages at the head of the prayers themselves. These passages are taken from the equivalent weeks of the previous calendar year, so that the theme of John's gospel is largely maintained.

The weeks fall into five sections shown by the running titles on the left hand pages.

Each week, the reader is invited to pray for a member church of the Council for World Mission or another ecumenical or religious organisation in Britain and Ireland. Addresses of these organisations are given on the appropriate pages. More information on CWM partner churches can be found in the centre pages of the book.

I have much enjoyed working with Michael and Susan, and with Craig. The prayer handbook committee, chaired by Debbie Reynolds, has taken a lively and sometimes uproarious interest in the preparation of the texts. Terry Oakley, who, as Secretary of Faith and Life, and more recently Secretary for Doctrine, Prayer and Worship of the United Reformed Church, has been secretary to the committee for eight years, has moved on. All who have used the handbook during those years owe a great debt to Terry for his sensitive leadership and his attention to detail. We will miss him.

A selection of prayers and other material on cassette can be obtained from the United Reformed Church. The text of the prayers is also available on computer disk in CP/M and MS-DOS versions. For details, contact Michael Durber, care of the Congregational Centre, 4 Castle Gate, Nottingham NG1 7AS.

Janet H. Wootton

Read: John 1.29-34

'I did not know who he was, but the reason why I came, baptising in water, was that he might be revealed to Israel.'

The stated aim of the fourth gospel is, 'that you may believe that Jesus is the Christ, the Son of God, and that through this faith you may have life by his name.' (20.31) To this end, those who have seen bear witness, beginning with John the baptiser.

John's great witness was that he had seen the Spirit coming down like a dove and resting on Jesus, and having seen, he bore witness. Again and again in John's gospel, witness and sight are linked. Jesus himself tells Nicodemus, 'we speak of what we know and testify to what we have seen' (3.11). And at the crucial point at the death of Jesus, the writer adds his own guarantee. When the soldier thrusts his spear into Jesus' side, blood and water flow from the wound, and 'This is vouched for by an eye-witness whose evidence is to be trusted. He knows that he speaks the truth, so that you too may believe.' (19.35)

The aim is belief. The seer bears witness so that those who hear may believe. The testimony of these witnesses is important, for there will be others who will not see Jesus, but will believe. They are the subject of Jesus' prayer in John 17.20 and of his blessing in 20.29.

John the Baptiser knows his place in the scheme of things. His purpose is to act in such a way that Jesus will be revealed. His task is simple. It is to look out for the sign of the Spirit, and, when he sees it to bear witness, becoming the first of that blessed generation of those who were eye-witnesses to the saving work of God.

Pray for: CCBI (Council of Churches for Britain and Ireland)
Interchurch House, 35-41 Lower Marsh, London SE1 7RL

I have seen it

A woman smiles with beauty and tenderness upon her child
and the tired and wise ones gaze
on his holy, wrinkled face.

Praise God! - They saw it and have borne witness.

A man walks at Bethany and someone sees the holy love of God.
This is the one who will forgive and carry
the sinfulness of all the world.

Praise God! - They saw it and have borne witness.

A dove rests on a man's shoulder
and it is the Holy Spirit in flight.
This is the one who will bring a new Spirit to fill our hearts!

Praise God! - They saw it and have borne witness.

A woman stands appalled before a cross
as the storm darkens and rages.
A man's blood falls upon the earth
and the ground shakes in terror.

Praise God! - They saw it and have borne witness.

A woman peers into an empty grave.
Angels ask why she weeps,
but the gardener knows and speaks her name.

Praise God! - They saw it and have borne witness.

Such moments have come to me, not the same, but different ones -
moments of 'epiphany',
of knowing more surely than I have ever known,
that you, my God, are here.

I have seen it and have borne witness. Amen.

Read: John 1.35-51

He turned and saw them following. 'What are you looking for?' he asked them. They said, 'Rabbi . . . where are you staying?' 'Come and see,' he replied, so they went and saw where he was staying.

'Staying' (sometimes translated 'dwelling' or 'abiding') and 'seeing' are important words in John's gospel. Like many pieces of dialogue in John, this can be interpreted at two levels. At one level, it is simply a request for personal information - where are you staying. But these are disciples of John the Baptist, whom he brings to Jesus, and Jesus' question, 'What are you looking for?' is the clue that there is another level of meaning.

Much, much later, the disciples of Jesus will be told of the importance of 'dwelling' in him, and in his love. Dwelling in Jesus is a pattern for living: it arises out of keeping his commands, and results in bearing much fruit.

But the greater emphasis here is on seeing, following John's witness when he saw the sign of the dove. 'Come and see,' says Jesus.

The two disciples, having seen the dwelling place of Jesus and found what they were looking for, go and tell others. Andrew calls his brother Peter, and Philip fetches Nathaniel. The chain of witness has begun. It is for us, who find our dwelling in Jesus, to tell what we have seen, and bear witness to the world that we have found the Messiah. We have found what we were looking for.

Martin Luther King Day (15th January)
Pray for: ACTS (Action of Churches Together in Scotland)
Scottish Churches House, Dunblane FK15 0AJ

Follow me

Can it be that easy?
Just two words – 'Follow me',
and without thinking what we are leaving behind
we go with you?

The simplicity and suddenness of it seem unbelievable.
I like to know what the cost will be
before I commit myself,
and I want to know where you will take me.
I'm comfortable in my familiar ways.
I like the safety of home.
The road may be too narrow,
too stony or too steep.
My heart is not so strong
and so easily breaks.
Persuade me with logic.
Convince me with miracles.
Let me see the reward up front,
and then maybe I'll go with you.
All I want is to make a sensible choice.
Maybe that's the problem.
With you, I really have no choice to make.
I am so used to wanting to be in control
that it is hard not to turn even my faith
into a carefully chosen commodity,
picked from the shelf,
selected for value, offering comfort.
But now the choice is yours.

You knew us before we knew ourselves.
By the sea, in church, under a tree
or on the road
you confront us with your presence
and we know we have to go with you.
Wherever the path leads,
it is enough
that we are going with you.

Read: John 2.1-11

'. . . but you have kept the best wine till now.'

Week of Prayer for Christian Unity
Pray for: CYTUN (Churches Together in Wales)
First Floor, 21 St Helen's Road, Swansea SA1 4AP

Water into wine

Glory to God when water turns to wine!

Thank you for the miracle of a good wine;
the grapes on sunny slopes,
the juice fermenting in the vat,
the nose and the flavours,
the colours and the tipsiness.
Thank you for the table wine, the fine wine,
the bubbly and the solemn wine.
Thank you for the freedom and the friendliness,
the passion and the pleasure,
of good and wonderful wine.

Glory to God when water turns to wine!

Thank you for the grace of sacrament and sign;
the water that washes and enlivens,
that brings new birth and new beginning,
the wine that makes glad the heart,
that shares in the death and life of Jesus.
Thank you for these holy signs,
making real your presence and your love.
Touching, tasting, bathing, drinking,
the water and the wine,
bring you here in splendour and in love.

Glory to God when water turns to wine!

Thank you for each miracle of transformation;
when tired and tepid lives find joy again,
when empty relationships are filled once more with love,
when struggle and poverty give way to plenty.
Thank you for the longing and the vision,
that one day all who now cry out in emptiness
will be filled to overflowing
and know that you have kept the best wine for them.

Glory to God when water turns to wine!

Read: John 2.13-25

He made a whip of cords and drove them out of the Temple.

Build up a picture in your mind's eye, and your mind's hand and nose. Think of the whip of cords. Look at it. Feel its texture, smell the tang of cord in your hands. This is a weapon of violence; of anger suddenly aroused and suddenly expressed.

If Jesus were suddenly present with you now, in the flesh, as he was present in the Temple, what would be his reaction to you? As you are a Temple of the Holy Spirit, would you disappoint him, like the Temple in Jerusalem? Would you feel the harshness of his judgment, and the lashing of his words?

If you could take the whiplash into the church today, where would you apply it? Do you react in anger to things that happen in your own church, or in the churches in your own country, or elsewhere in the world? Do you think your anger is justified, as Jesus' was?

Now look further. Is this sudden anger justifiably aroused by what we are doing to God's world and the people in it? Are there forces at work in the world which are as blasphemous as the practices of the money-changers and sellers of sacrifices in the Temple?

In the other gospels, this act of Jesus comes much later in his ministry. John places it almost at the beginning. It is Jesus' first act of defiance against the power-bases of his day, and became the first round in a constant conflict with them. Do we have the right and the courage to share his anger?

Pray for: The Churches Together in England
Interchurch House, 35-41 Lower Marsh, London SE1 7RL

Turn over the tables

**God of truth,
come again to the places of learning
and turn over the tables
on those who exploit, deceive
or constrict the truth.**

When the place where we are born
determines the quality of education.

When money can buy learning
which is your gift for us all.

When children are not encouraged
and gifts are not recognised.

When parents can provide no good example.

When religion obscures truth,
leaders become hypocrites
and no one objects.

When faith becomes unthinking
and reason is rejected.

When learning is despised
and truth is prostituted.

When access to education is restricted
because of ability, race, class or health.

*(Add examples of where tables should be overturned from your own
experiences of learning.)*

**God of truth,
come again to the places of learning
and turn over the tables
on those who exploit, deceive
or constrict the truth.**

Read: John 8.21-36

Turning to the Jews who had believed in him . . .

Jesus addresses two audiences. There are 'the Jews' who are largely hostile and unbelieving, and, among them, 'the Jews who have believed'. The unbelievers are judged and will die in their sins. But the believers have the chance to be set free, to be set free by the truth and be free indeed.

The division is not permanent. People move between the two groups. Nicodemus, for example, is one of the Pharisees, a group largely hostile. On the other hand, the teaching following the miraculous feeding causes a mass exodus, leaving, perhaps, only the Twelve (John 6.66).

The distinction is not clear either. Jesus' harshest words in this part of his teaching are reserved for the believing Jews. It is they who are the children of the Devil, and full of his murderous intentions.

Even we, who believe, may expect to hear harsh words of judgment from Jesus. To be a follower is not a licence for self-satisfaction or complacency, but it is the chance of freedom.

Education Sunday
Pray for: The Free Church Federal Council
27 Tavistock Square, London WC1H 9HH

Love and judgement

I have much to say about you – and in judgement.

Jesus,
what would you say in judgement about me?
Would you have much to say,
a long speech naming each hidden guilt,
prodding my shame, making me wince?
Would you be gentle,
more gentle with me than I am with myself?
Would you, knowing all things,
be more forgiving of me than I can be?
Would you punish me or set me free,
make me suffer or make me better?

You will know the truth, and the truth will set you free.

Jesus,
show me the truth about myself and set me free.
I want to know where my faults lie
and where I need to change my ways.
I am afraid of what is in me,
of my past and present sinfulness,
the wrong I do not want to admit
and the failings I know all too well.
Show me where goodness lives in me,
where gracefulness and love make me worthy to be yours.
Let me not think too badly of myself
but let me see the truth of who I am.
Make me better. Set me free.

You will indeed be free.

Jesus,
I choose with longing your gifts of forgiveness and freedom.
Let me live with you all my days,
your disciple, standing by your teaching, embracing life.
And may I be as gentle and liberating in my judgement of others,
as you have been of me.

Read: John 5. 1-18

. . . a man who had been crippled for thirty-eight years.

Thirty-eight years ago, it was February 11th 1958. The post-war era was just ending, and the 1960s were beginning to heave into view. Teen-agers had just become an economic and social group. Many of our streets were still safe.

In a group, or on your own, consider what you were doing thirty-eight years ago. Perhaps you were not born. Perhaps you were at school, or beginning a career, or bringing up children. If you had been crippled for all those years, what would you not have achieved? 'Crippled' might include a physical condition, or something which prevented you from living a full life - lack of money, homelessness, emotional or spiritual depression.

You may indeed have known a period which you would describe as 'crippled'. Others in a group might be willing to share such an experience. On the other hand, some may be living with a condition which others regard as 'crippling', but which they regard in quite a different light.

What are the forces that cripple people's lives in our time? How can Jesus' followers reach out with the love of Jesus to those who no longer have the power to reach out for themselves?

Pray for: The Presbyterian Church of Myanmar

No one to help

Pray today for those who wait,
especially those who wait alone.

*Name in God's presence people who are waiting –
for example, those who wait:*

- for a job which never comes
- for a chance to prove their worth
- for renewal in the church
- for political change
- for release from bonded labour
- for healing
- for the results of a hospital test
- for a child
- for death
- for a home
- for someone to love

In silence, wait on God, who hears our prayers.

Living God,
while we wait for others to help
you come yourself.
Seen or unseen,
in loud distress or in silent trust,
you know the way we take.
You crush our misplaced hope
and make us strong.
In our trials,
you will bring joy.

Read: John 6.1-15

They gathered them up, and filled twelve baskets with the pieces of the five barley loaves that were left uneaten.

This is what happens when Jesus wants to display a sign of God's power and love. There is a superabundance: six huge stone jars of water were turned into wine, and wine of the highest quality; the officer's son was healed without Jesus even meeting him; and now there is enough bread left over from the five loaves, after five-thousand people have been fed, to fill twelve baskets with the pieces.

The figure twelve is important. There are twelve chosen disciples, and twelve baskets to take away from the feast. When God's people trust in God, not only do miracles happen, but there is a superabundance of grace. There is enough for every disciple to carry into the world of need.

But there are far more than five thousand now who need feeding, both physically and spiritually. The hungry, in both senses, crowd our doors and fill the world. The miracle is still to come.

Pray for:
The United Congregational Church of Southern Africa

Bread from heaven

God,
we long for bread from heaven,
a miracle to feed the countless hungry ones
whose despair eats at our compassion
and whose anger leaves us tasting a bitter guilt.
Couldn't you do it again,
even just once,
to fill the empty stomachs and to quieten the cries?
If only they could all have as much they wanted,
with no more suffering, no more death;
if only there could be nothing wasted,
no grain mountains, no rotting, stale uneaten waste.
Give us bread from heaven!

God,
we have only bread from earth,
grain grown in the soil,
milled by our labour,
bread made by human hands,
bought and sold in our markets
and traded at our rates.
What is this among so many?
Give us bread from heaven!

God,
there is no manna now,
no free lunch.
Do not tease us with miracles.
Show us, instead,
how to make bread from earth,
so that all people
will have
enough.

Read: John 13. 31-35

'I give you a new commandment: love one another; as I have loved you, so you are to love one another. If there is this love in you, then everyone will know that you are my disciples.'

This is quite different from the great commandment of the synoptic gospels: 'You shall love the Lord your God with all your heart, with all your soul, with all your mind and with all your strength', and 'You shall love your neighbour as yourself.' These are old commands, in the sense that they are quotations from the Law of Moses, from Deuteronomy and Leviticus. The command to 'love one another' is new.

The old commands are general. They are ways to achieve the fulfilment of all the Law. The new command is specific to the believers, and describes a mutual bond. The model for the bond is the love of Jesus for the disciples, and the purpose is witness to those who are not, as yet, within the bond of Christian love. It is to be the mark by which the disciples of Jesus are to be known.

Unemployment Sunday
Pray for: CAP
(Church Action on Poverty)
Central Buildings, Oldham
Street, Manchester M1 1JT

Love for one another   John 13.31-35

Let us hold fast to our confession.   Hebrews 4.14

**God's love was revealed among us in this way:
God sent his only Son into the world so that we might live
through him.**   1 John 4.9

You shall love the Lord your God with all your heart, and with all
your soul and with all your might. You shall love your neighbour
as yourself.   Deuteronomy 6.5; Leviticus 19.17

**Let us clothe ourselves with love, which binds everything
together in perfect harmony.**   Colossians 3.14

You shall love the alien as yourself, for you were aliens in the land
of Egypt.   Leviticus 19.34

**Let us love one another with mutual affection, outdo one
another in showing honour. We will contribute to the
needs of the saints and extend hospitality to strangers.**
                                                  Romans 12.10,13

Love your enemies and pray for those who persecute you.
                                                     Matthew 5.44
**Christ is our peace; he has broken down the dividing wall,
that is, the hostility between us. Let us pursue peace with
everyone.**   Ephesians 1.14; Hebrews 12.14

Love is strong as death, passion as fierce as the grave.
                                               Song of Solomon 8.6
**Neither death, nor life, nor angels, nor rulers, nor things
present, nor things to come, nor powers, nor height, nor
depth, nor anything else in all creation, will be able to
separate us from the love of God in Christ Jesus our Lord.**
                                                  Romans 8.38-39

Just as I have loved you, you also should love one another.
                                                     John 13.34
**So let us put away all bitterness and wrath and anger and
wrangling and slander, together with all malice, and be
kind to one another, tender-hearted, forgiving one
another as God in Christ has forgiven us.**   Ephesians 4.31-32

Biblical texts are adapted from the NRSV.

Read: John 9: (1-12) 13-41

Jesus said, 'It is for judgment that I have come into this world – to give sight to the sightless and to make blind those who see.'

You may like to carry out this exercise:

In a group, let everybody close their eyes. People wearing glasses may like to remove them. At one point in the circle, or at one end of each line, one person should lay his/her hands on the eyes of his/her neighbour. This is a gentle and loving action, and when the hands are removed, the neighbour opens his/her eyes, and turns to the next person to lay on hands, and so on till all (including the first person) have their eyes open.

In a large group, people could begin singing a simple chant (for example, 'O Lord hear my prayer' from Taizé) as their eyes are opened. The song then spreads round the room as the eyes are opened.

If you are alone, simply sit for a while with your eyes closed, contemplating the words of Jesus, then open your eyes, and look around you, giving thanks for what you see.

In what sense does Jesus make blind, as well as giving sight?

If you, or a member of the group is physically blind, or partially sighted, any discussion should include the reality and value of this experience.

Pray for: The Presbyterian Church of Wales

Seeing and not seeing

Jesus,
I wish it did not seem so easy for you.
You forgive a sinner
and he is forgiven.
You heal a woman
and she is healed.
Even with the man born blind,
it takes just mud and spit
and a wash in the pool of Siloam.
My attempts at forgiving are so faltering
and I'm tempted to leave healing to the doctors.
It takes just a word from you,
while we must draw up an agenda,
talk out a meeting,
organise a feasibility study.
Am I too impatient?
Can you understand our questions,
our debate and hesitation?
Can you accept our failures?
I wish it didn't seem so easy for you.
You put me to shame.
Except you too were put to shame,
closing your eyes in death.

Jesus,
I am blind.
Help me to see
how you can forgive me.

Help me to see.

Read: John 6. 60-71

On hearing this, some of the disciples exclaimed, 'This is more than we can stand! How can anyone listen to such talk?'

The translation has lost something. The phrase *more than we can stand*, is the translation of one word - 'skleros', meaning 'hard' or 'stiff'. Here was the point at which the going got too tough even for the disciples. The teaching of Jesus was hard, intractable.

Jesus' word back to them is also important. He says, 'Does this shock you?' The Greek is 'skandalizei?': are you scandalised, or are you offended?

Both these words are important in scripture, though in very different writings from John's gospel. The skandalos was the stumbling block which the crucifixion of Christ formed for the Jews (I Cor 1.23), preventing them from believing. As in this 'hard' teaching, it is the sacrifice of Christ, the consumption of the bread from heaven, which forms a sticking point.

But it is not the teaching which is skleros, hard or intractable. For the writer to the Hebrews, quoting the Greek form of Psalm 95, it is the hearts of those who will not believe. For this writer, the chance only comes 'Today', when you 'hear God's voice'. At that moment our hearts may harden or stiffen in rebellion against God's words. We may come crashing down on the stumbling block and go no further.

Or, like Peter and the rest of the Twelve, we may recognise the echo of truth in the voice of God. Our hearts may be softened and, hard as it is, we may respond.

Pray for:
The United Church of Jamaica and the Cayman Islands

To whom shall we go?

God who made us,
some of us long for a God
who had made things differently,
a world with no pain,
with more beauty and equality,
with less mystery and less terror.
But there is no other God.
To whom shall we go?

God in Jesus,
some of us long for a different Christ,
one more to our taste and for our times,
a woman Christ, a white Christ,
a helpful Christ who did not die such a death.
But you came as you did.
To whom shall we go?

Holy Spirit,
some of us long for you to renew all people,
to make everyone laugh and sing
and know no fear
or have no need to struggle hard for truth.
But you move secretly and subtly.
To whom shall we go?

God, you are not always the one we desire.
Where is your swift justice?
When were you born in the form of a woman?
Why do you hide yourself from us?
Some have left,
some of us are tempted to leave,
for a good reason,
to find a better God.
But, to whom shall we go?
Yours are the words of eternal life.

Read: John 12. 1-8

*Then Mary brought a pound of very costly perfume, pure oil of nard,
and anointed Jesus's feet and wiped them with her hair, till the house
was filled with the fragrance.*

Perfume is still an extravagant present for a man or a woman.
All the toiletries with which we bathe or anoint our bodies carry a
perfume or fragrance, which is designed to enhance or override the
natural smell of the body. As such, perfume is a luxury, almost the
epitomy of luxury. What is the use of a lovely smell?

In a sense, however, scent is the most generous of gifts. The pure
nard poured out by Mary soon filled the house with its fragrance.
All that luxury and decadence was evident to the servants in the
hall as well as the diners at the feast. No-one could escape the
all-pervading scent, borne on the air.

So powerful is the scent that its offence is immediate. Judas, vilified
by John, bristles with the obvious response. 'What a waste!' All
that money diffused in air. Surely it could have been better used.
What about the poor, whose smell is quite different? What about
the poor, who have no resources to waste on such fripperies?

Let your sense of smell tell you about this story. Savour the meal,
the proximity of people, then, first the hint and then the
overpowering scent of nard.

Mothering Sunday
Pray for: CWM Women's Advisory Group

Sensing love

God, you are warm and close to me,
as the smell of my mother's body
and the loving strength of her embrace.

God, you stir my desire and awaken my senses,
as the pleasure of beauty in a face,
and the scent of my own true love.

God, I am filled with longing for you,
as I hunger for warm bread
and the taste of the sun in scented wine.

God, my heart is stirred to heaven,
as I hear the beats of a jazz theme
or the melody of a high romantic symphony.

God, my prayer rises to heaven,
as the incense cloud fills the room
and I breathe deep the smell of holiness.

God, who has given me senses
for pain and for delight,
let me take pleasure in my body,
that I may anticipate the joy
of knowing you.

Read: John 12. 20-36

'*The hour has come for the Son of Man to be glorified.*'

For a long time, the hour had not come. There is a sense of waiting for the right time. The whole gospel is leading up to the hour. Look at John 2.4, for example, where Jesus' words to his mother are based on the fact that 'my hour has not yet come.'

When it comes, it is the hour for the *Son of Man*. This strange expression has a long history in Scripture. In the Hebrew Scriptures, each man was 'son of', and each woman, 'daughter of' a family, a tribe, and eventually the people of Israel. The Israelites were the 'children of Israel'. This fixed their place in the human race.

But the phrase 'son of man' came to mean, not a member of a family or tribe, but a member of the human race. It seems to have been used as a general term, and as a symbolic term. The Son of Man in Daniel 7.22 is interpreted as the saints of the Most High. He is a figure who incorporates humanity.

This, then, is the hour for that focal human being, the crucial hour for the whole human race.

It is the hour for the Son of Man *to be glorified*. For John, the moment of crucifixion was the glorification, the exaltation of Jesus. After the hour has come, nothing is ever the same again, for anyone.

Pray for: Gereja Presbyterian Malaysia

The hour has come

The hour has come -
the hour of strange wisdom,
where death is trampled
by life which is lost,
stained in the press
of victory's defeat.

May the name of Jesus Christ be glorified on earth.

The hour has come -
the hour of the cold earth,
a seed alone in death,
bearing the germ, the life,
the fruit.

May the name of Jesus Christ be glorified on earth.

The hour has come -
the hour when rulers are disarmed,
the nails, the spear
the power, mockery
shamed and shattered;
and deceit is destroyed
by God's pain.

May the name of Jesus Christ be glorified on earth.

The hour has come -
the hour of glory,
when we are raised with Christ,
lifted and carried by the dead saviour,
spattered and stained
by God's lifeblood.

May the name of Jesus Christ be glorified on earth.

The hour has come.

Read: John 18. 1–40

. . . they shouted back, 'Not him; we want Barabbas!'

Pray for: The Kiribati Protestant Church

Palm Sunday

Where we stand

R/ Jesus, we stand before you.

We stand with the great crowd at the festival,
we shout hosanna
and praise you as the coming king,
the answer to our dreams.   **R/**

We stand with Judas in the garden,
siding with the police and chief priests,
selling out to power and money,
betraying you to violence.   **R/**

We stand with Peter, trying to be loyal,
but getting it wrong, not ready for defeat,
fighting back with bloodshed and deceit,
though you must drink the cup and die. **R/**

We stand with Pilate in the praetorium,
trying to escape the choice between good and bad,
shuttling between diplomacy and truth,
abdicating to a crowd.   **R/**

We stand with soldiers to mock and gamble round the cross,
following instructions,
and looking to ourselves
while you look down on us as king.   **R/**

We stand with Mary, pierced by grief,
but finding at the cross
the love that had seemed lost
and the beginning of our faith.   **R/**

As Easter people,
we cannot pretend
that you are not risen,
but today we stand within the shadow of your cross.

R/ Jesus, we stand before you.

Read: John 13.1-30

It was night.

Now the night has come, long-foreseen by Jesus, in which no-one can walk or work. Throughout John's gospel, there has been a constant sense of urgency, for the day is passing, and the night will surely come. This short chilling sentence describes not only the literal darkness of the night in which Jesus was betrayed, but also the symbolic darkness brought on by Judas' act.

In the Hebrew Scriptures, darkness is the uncreated chaos from which God divided the newly created light (Genesis 1.4). It is the time of mystery, through which Jacob wrestled with God and prevailed (Genesis 33.22-32). It is the darkness in which people walk before the great light of God's promise shines on them (Isaiah 9.2, 60.1-2). And, finally, it is banished for ever from the new Jerusalem (Isaiah 60.19-20).

But there is another story. The Hebrew Scriptures are always complex, and every image is interwoven with its opposite. Here the darkness is the dwelling place of God, wrapping God in unknowable mystery.

When Solomon held his great spectacular opening for the new Temple, the priests were driven out of the Holy Place by the glory of the LORD - not bright light, but cloud. Solomon was driven to proclaim, 'The Lord has caused his sun to shine in the heavens, but he has said he would dwell in thick darkness' (I Kings 8.12). Similarly, the prophet Ezekiel's terrifying vision of God includes not only flashing light, but also storm clouds (Ezekiel 1.4), and the Psalmist knows that the night is no hiding place from God (Psalm 139.11-12).

> Now, as Judas walks out into the night,
> Jesus leaves the day behind, and God enters
> the familiar dark.

Pray for: Other churches in the area in which you live

Unsafe places

God of all love,
you take the risk of inviting us in
to share your supper.
You call us your friends.
Bread and wine are given for our comfort.
But the very place of our fellowship
becomes the table of betrayal.
We cannot keep faith with you.
>   And it is night.

We take the risk
of opening our table
and find our hospitality flung back in our face,
our property taken,
our care despised.
>   And it is night.

We take the risk
of loving each other
as you commanded.
But our love is betrayed
and our commitment too fickle.
Our promises turn to dust.
>   And it is night.

We take the risk
of going out with you into the dark street
but we have stayed inside too long
and cannot survive outside the prison
we have built for our souls.
>   And it is night.

You take the risk
of making a new deal –
a covenant sealed with forgiveness.
>   As night falls
>   you go with us into that familiar dark.

Read: John 19.17-37

Ways of looking.

You may like to base a period of meditation on the hymn of Isaac Watts, 'When I survey the wondrous cross'.

First read, or sing the hymn. You may be singing it as part of a Good Friday act of worship. Begin the meditation from verses three and four, which focus on the visual impact of Jesus on the cross.

Let the images from John's very plain description of the crucifixion give content to the rich imagery of the hymn. What are the sorrow and love which flow mingled down?

Let your mind come to a rest at the end of verse four.

Then move to the intensely personal language of verses one and two. This is not simply a descriptive hymn about the death of Jesus; it is what happens when I survey it. Let your mind range over your own richest gain, the vain things that charm you most, your boasting and pride.

Verse five gathers the thought of the hymn into a simple and powerful act of commitment. You may like to make it your own act of commitment, or, in the context of a group or congregation, make a corporate act at this point.

Pray for: your local ecumenical group or groups

Look on him

Show us, God, what we do not want to see
and yet must see.
Let us look upon the one they pierced.

Show us the places of execution,
the torture chambers and the prisons,
where skulls are crushed and minds distorted.

Show us the truth about brutality and violence,
about unjust sentences and miscarriages of justice,
when someone's quibble is another's death or life.

Show us the weeping and the agony
of the family and the friends,
the ones who, in their love, can only watch.

Show us the corpses, broken and bleeding.
Show us what humankind has accomplished in its fury.
Let us see, so that we may know it is true.

Show us, God, what we do not want to see
and yet must see.
Let us look upon the ones they pierced.

And as we look, in terror and reproach,
can we know that it is you we see,
bearing the pain we dread,
sharing the injustice,
suffering the humiliation?
For only so, could we bear to look.

Read: John 20.1-18

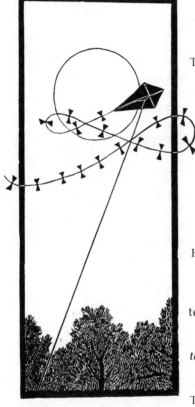

She turned round and saw Jesus standing there, but she did not recognise him. Jesus asked her, 'Why are you weeping?'

The angels have already asked Mary this question, and her answer is the same in both cases, that she is weeping because they have taken Jesus away - not his body, you understand, but 'my Lord', or 'him'. She has come to show her love for Jesus in the traditional task of laying him out for burial. She will touch his body again, be near him again. But even this is denied her.

Her grief blinds her. Although she is first at the tomb, she, unlike Peter and the beloved disciple, does not see. Even when she sees Jesus, her tear-filled eyes cannot take in who it is. First she *hears*, 'Mary', then she turns, but is still not allowed to *touch*. 'Do not cling!' must have been unbearably hard words.

Then she is sent as the apostle to the apostles, the first with the message - at last she can say, '*I have seen*'. Peter and the beloved disciple see nothing and believe. Mary, however, has seen the Lord.

Pray for: The local church in which you worship

Isaiah 55.1-11;
I Corinthians 5.7b-8;
John 20.1-18

Easter

Easter Sunday

We thank you God for this amazing day,
when our hearts dance like the shining sun,
when all the world leaps with life
and the great, infinite wonders of the earth
shout their 'yes!' to you.

We who have seen death,
who have heard the story of the cross
and sorrowed deep at the sharp agony of the world's pain,
we have come to life again
in the life of your Son.

With Christ we have been lifted from the nothing of death
into your new and unimagined life,
where tasting, touching, hearing, seeing and breathing,
are more sweet than we had known before
and where you are in beauty and in truth.
How could we ever doubt you,
when today your Spirit makes us dance and shout,
to the praise of the risen one,
the one who has defeated death and all the evil powers?
How could we doubt you,
now that our ears are awake and our eyes are opened?

We thank you God for this amazing day,
when the evil in us lies down dead,
and the good in us is born again.
This is the birth day of life and love and goodness.
This is the amazing day,
when our Saviour rose, when the earth released him,
when the heavens echoed the praise of earth, on this great day.
Alleluia! to our leaping, rising, lively, infinite, God.

This prayer was inspired by the reading from John's Gospel
and by a sonnet by e.e. cummings: *i thank you God for most this amazing day*.

Read: John 20. 19-31

Jesus said again, 'Peace be with you! As the Father sent me, so I send you.' Then he breathed on them, saying, 'Receive the Holy Spirit! If you forgive anyone's sins, they are forgiven; if you pronounce them unforgiven, unforgiven they remain.'

This is a terrifying commission. How dare we, the disciples of Jesus, take up the power of forgiveness, or, worse, unforgiveness? What sins would we pronounce unforgiven for ever?

> Meditate alone, or discuss together, how the gift of the Holy Spirit and the sending (apostolate) conferred by the Father upon Jesus and by Jesus upon the disciples, bears on the power to give or withold forgiveness. Do you, or members of the group, have any experience which touches on this awesome responsibility?

Pray for: The Presbyterian Church of Southern Africa

Easter faith

This is the faith which we share.

With the Roman centurion who helped crucify you,
We confess you are "God's Son."

With Peter who denied you three times,
We believe "You are the Messiah, the Son of the living God."

With Thomas who doubted you,
We declare, "My Lord and my God."

With Paul who persecuted you,
We proclaim "Jesus Christ, and him crucified."

With Martha whose brother Lazarus had died,
We believe "You are the Messiah, the Son of God."

With Mary of Magdala who wept at the tomb and met her risen saviour,
We announce the good news: "I have seen the Lord!"

Quotations are from:
Mark 15.39; Matthew 16.16; John 20.28; I Corinthians 2.2; John 11.27; John 20.18

Read: John 21.1-14

'Jesus said, 'Come and have breakfast.' None of the disciples dared to ask, 'Who are you?' They knew it was the Lord.

Imagine the smell of fish cooking over an open fire, the texture and taste of bread, the fresh light and air of early morning. Find words to describe the sights, tastes and smells. In a group or congregational setting, brainstorm the words and let them fill the air. If the setting includes food - refreshments or communion - let the real food and drink be present - the smell of communion wine or coffee, the anticipated taste of bread or biscuits.

Imagine a meal eaten with friends with whom a task has been shared, hungry together, satisfied with work done. Let a new set of words describe the sensation. There may be specific occasions you, or some in the group or congregation can remember.

This is a sacrament, a sacrament of friendship, communion/breakfast in bread and fish - the food of miracles. Dare you ask the identity of the one who is present in the sharing of friends, who is dead and yet is alive, who is as real as the food we eat and the love we share?

In a moment of quietness, acknowledge the presence of Jesus. In the wonder of his presence, we dare not ask - we know.

Pray for: The Presbyterian Church in Taiwan

Breakfast on the beach

Lord, there are times when there's nothing doing.
Even so soon after your resurrection,
when we'd got our courage back
and lived for a while just with the wonder of it,
we're back in the routine,
being frustrated,
fishing in the dark and getting nothing -
> empty pews again,
> empty hearts too, love ebbing,
> and hollow stomachs, too many by far.
We confess our failure.

Then you tell us to go again,
to look elsewhere,
and the result overwhelms us.
This isn't what we'd expected.
In places we'd not looked,
> your church grows,
> our joy returns,
> and food is given.
We revel in your provision
and struggle to take it in.

Now we look into your eyes
as we learn again to share food round a table
and we're stumped for words.
We'd not expected it.
Even here, in this place,
> in the kitchen,
> on the beach,
> down the road with our friends,
you invite us to your breakfast
and we see how you can feed us.
The day breaks,
light returns.
It's resurrection day again.

Read: John 21. 15-25

There is much else that Jesus did. If it were all to be recorded in detail, I suppose the world could not hold the books that would be written

The book was the information break-through of the early years of the Christian era. It was capable of holding more information in a more accessible form than the scroll.

Today, the British Library contains about twenty million books housed in buildings scattered around London. They take up some 340 miles of shelving.

If the same information were contained on Compact Discs, they could be held on about 700 yards of shelving - they would line the walls of a large front room.

Interactive teaching programmes now make it possible not just to read about, but to hear recordings and see pictures and videos of events.

Yet, the full story of the life of Jesus is still being told, not merely in books or other technologies, but in human lives and renewed communities. The world has proved too small to hold all that Jesus is doing and has done.

Praise God for the living record of the living Christ.

Pray for: The Church Computer Users Group
Revd Stoker Wilson, St John's Vicarage, Greenside, Ryton, Tyne & Wear NE40 4AA

A pattern for our living

Let the food from the table
    make us strong to answer hunger.

Let the care from the shepherd
    make us quick to love God's people.

Let the questions which have challenged us
    overcome our denial.

Let the call from your voice
    find an answer in our heart.

Now we hold our hands out to you,
    and you take us where we do not want to go.

Jesus, there is so much more to know of you,
not yet written down.
The story is not ended,
    but we will write it in our lives.

Read: John 15.18-27

'If the world hates you, it hated me first, as you know well.'

God forgive us

'As far as I am concerned, what I see in religion is not the mystery of the Incarnation but a mystery of the social order: it prevents the rich from being massacred by the poor by relating the idea of equality to heaven . . .'

'Priests are worth more than Kant and all the German dreamers put together. Without religion, how could we have order in the state? Society cannot continue to exist without inequalities of personal fortunes; for inequalities to continue we must have religion. When someone is dying of hunger and someone else nearby has everything, it would be impossible for the starving man to acquiesce to disparity if there were no authority to tell him: God wills it so; in this world there must be rich and poor but in the hereafter for all eternity, fortunes will be reversed.'

Napoleon Bonaparte

Pray for: The SCM Press Trust
26-30 Tottenham Road, London N1 4BZ

Love's opposite: indifference

God, to have the world's indifference seems far worse to me than
to have its hatred. I look back longingly on times when Christians
were important enough to be hated, stoned and spat upon.
Wouldn't that be preferable to the gradual and sinking decay that
seems to have overcome us now?

God, let me take you to a church in the inner city. It used to be a
thriving centre of community life. It has still a huge building;
five storeys of rooms and halls and kitchens. The worship used to
take place in a large hall at the centre. It was fine in its day; with
a gentle blue ceiling and white plasterwork. Now the worship still
goes on, in a smaller room, but there used to be fifty times today's
number of worshippers with an orchestra and fine singers in the
choir. Come with me into the large hall which still lies derelict at
the heart of the building, the plaster falling off the ceiling and
walls, the windows bricked up against vandals, the pews sold and
the floor dusty and unswept. An old bath stands in one corner.
A fragment of vine can still be seen carved on a pillar, but there
is nothing living and bearing fruit here now. The church has
retreated into a small room and worries about its future. And all
around the church building, the city carries on its life and the
world beyond turns and turns and pays no attention to the church,
for what is there to fear or to love in such a sorry remnant of
something that was once significant?

Gentle God, if this is the trouble and persecution we must bear then
it is as terrible to us as the stoning or the spitting, the flames or the
lions. For while our bodies survive, our souls are destroyed. For I
know that this church is but a parable for all churches which face
the indifference of a laughing world as they tumble into emptiness.
God, how can I live your gospel in such times?

**God,
who in your son Jesus
faced hatred and opposition,
give us courage to face the world's indifference,
and, if we do not belong to the world,
assure us that we belong always to you.
Amen.**

Read: John 16. 25-33

'When that day comes you will make your request in my name, and I do not say that I shall pray to the Father for you, for the Father loves you himself, because you have loved me and believed that I came from God.'

All prayer flows on a current of love, and is held in a circle of love. This prayer handbook is only words. If the love is not there, these are not prayers. Prayer is the act of making the request in Jesus' name. By this, we demonstrate our belief in Jesus, and enter into the Father's love.

> Spend some time in quiet, considering your deepest requests for yourself, for the world, for the people you love.
>
> Spend some time putting your request in your own words. In a group, this may be a moment for open prayer, or for one person to gather up the prayers of others.

It takes courage to bring our deepest concerns to God's love, for they seem too much, or too little, to ask.

Pray for: The Scottish Congregational Church

Take courage

When we are ready to give up;
when the church doors close for the last time
and no one wants to know us,
Jesus says:
Take courage, I have conquered the world.

When our sisters and brothers have their lives taken;
when we cry for those we cannot help
and our voice goes unheard,
Jesus says:
Take courage, I have conquered the world.

When churches conspire with state and forget your demands;
when we despair at our complicity
and hide away our shame,
Jesus says:
Take courage, I have conquered the world.

When we are shunned by our friends and taunted by enemies;
when we are so keen to be wanted that we do what we despise
and forget where loyalty lies,
Jesus says:
Take courage, I have conquered the world.

When we forget our dignity;
when we think ourselves unlovely
and when we long for our pain to be changed into joy,
Jesus says:
Take courage, I have conquered the world.

Read: John 7. 32-39

'You will look for me but you will not find me; and where I am you cannot come.'

Earlier in John 7, the curious crowds have been looking for Jesus, wondering whether he will come to Jerusalem for the Feast. Later, the Pharisees send the temple police to look for him, in order to arrest him. Now Jesus points to a time when he will not be simply hidden among the crowd, but removed from them, in fact, by death. They will look, but he will no longer be available to the curious or the hostile.

Only those who believe will know, not where, but how to look. In the great farewell discourses, when Jesus is preparing his disciples for his death, he says, 'In a little while, the world will see me no longer, but you will see me; because I live, you will live.' (14.19)

(Music for these words can be found at back of book)

Some days the fog comes creeping
From mountains of my doubting,
And question marks climb peering
Through windows of my soul:
Asking, stealing,
Fighting in my mind.

If I could tell the mountains:
'Be moved into the ocean' -
The sea of God's own loving
Would wash into my soul:
Touching, healing
Eyes that seem so blind.

And I shall go on seeking,
For there must be an answer
In such a world of wonder
Where beauty lifts the soul:
Searching, Feeling -
'Seek and you will find.'

Cecily Taylor (1930 -)
Reproduced by permission of Stainer & Bell Ltd and
Women in Theology from 'Reflecting Praise'.

Christian Aid week
Pray for: Christian Aid Interchurch House, 35-41 Lower Marsh, London SE1 7RL, **SCIAF (Scottish Catholic International Aid Fund)** 5 Oswald Street, Glasgow G1 4QR **and CAFOD (Catholic Fund for Overseas Development)** Romero Close, Stockwell Road, London SW9 9TY

Love from within

Let us pray for those who have looked for Jesus
but have not found him.

Pray for the hungry and the homeless,
and for the grieving and the lonely ones.
Pray for those unjustly treated or falsely accused,
and for the prisoners and the dispossessed.
Pray for the slaves and the poorest of the poor,
for the desperate and for those without hope.

Let us pray for those who have looked for Jesus
but have not found him.

Pray for the women frightened of violent men,
and for the children who must keep terrible secrets.
Pray for the men who find it hard to weep,
and for the women who have little to make them laugh.
Pray for parents separated from their children
and for children who do not know they are loved.

Let us pray for those who have looked for Jesus
but have not found him.

Pray for the refugees and the landless,
and for all people who have no voice or vote in their own country.
Pray for those who cannot read or write,
and for all who are denied the power of knowledge and skill.
Pray for those whose bodies are damaged by war or pollution,
and for the mentally ill or tormented ones.

Let us pray for those who have looked for Jesus
but have not found him.

Loving Jesus, when we cannot find you,
show us the wells of living water within ourselves,
that we may find love to mend our own woes
and to heal the wounds of all the world. Amen.

Read: John 14.15-27

'Peace is my parting gift to you . . . .'

John's gospel is full of hints of the Spirit's coming. Nicodemus is told what it is like to be born of the Spirit; the woman at the well hears of a mysterious living water; Jesus proclaims the same living water from the Temple steps at the Festival of Tabernacles, with the proviso that the coming of the Spirit will be the moment when the Son of Man is glorified.

It is here, as he prepares for that glorification, which is his death, that Jesus talks most about the promised Spirit - the advocate and guide - but here, most of all, the accompaniment of the gift of peace. Jesus is preparing his disciples for the grief and sorrow which will accompany his death. Although it will seem like it, he will not be abandoning them.

But now, and in the future, when they must face the world's hatred, face persecution, face anxiety and trouble, which is only going to get worse, what the disciples are promised is peace.

Pray for: The United Church in Papua New Guinea and the Solomon Islands

Be with me

Be with me today, Holy Spirit of God,
be with me in the loving,
as I have another go at keeping your commands.

I know what it is to be considered weak,
to be thought a fool,
to be rejected by the world -
when no one applauds me
and my words are met by deafness.

I've heard all you've said
about washing each other's feet
and loving one another -
and I still want to do it,
but somehow I need your reassurance
that it's not all futile,
that we're not on our own.

So be with me today, Holy Spirit of God,
be with me in the loving.
Don't leave me orphaned
but come and make your home here with me,
and let me love again.

Let me understand more of you,
and give me your peace,
so that as you live,
I too may live for you.

Spirit of God,
fill me with your love.

Jesus says:
Peace I leave with you;
my peace I give to you.
I do not give to you as the world gives.
Do not let your hearts be troubled,
and do not let them be afraid.

Read: John 14.8-17

If you knew me you would know my Father too. From now on you do know him, you have seen him.

See if you can get hold of a computer generated 3-D picture. There are plenty of these around. In a group, perhaps one member could bring a book of them. They are computer generated images which present at first glance a confusion of minute detail. The first thing that becomes clear is that the detail is repeated - there is a kind of pattern. But the pattern is only a hint of the real nature of the picture. To perceive this takes a complete shift of focus, and is very hard to do. The trick is to lengthen the focus of the eyes, to look *through* the intricate and intriguing detail, and sometimes, not always, a 3D image jumps into startling clarity.

The effect is dramatic, and worth perseverance. When someone has looked and looked at 3-D images without effect, and suddenly sees one, he or she reacts with wonder and pleasure - 'I can see it!'. For a moment, the complete image is there, simple and startling. Then your focus returns to the surface of the picture, and the image dissolves into a mass of detail again.

It is not known whether there are people who are incapable of ever seeing the 3-D image, which is, of course, where the analogy breaks down, but it is interesting that people with poor eyesight seem to find it easier than those whose sight for normal seeing is perfect.

Pray for: The Church of South India

Trinity

I am tired of the negative way.
I am bored with unsaying.
I know what you are not.

I want to know what you are.

Immortal,
invisible,
unapproachable,
ineffable,
impassible -

these words tell me little.
They tell me what you are not,
but what are you?

I must say and unsay,
I must speak in riddles
and metaphor and paradox and puzzle,
of three in one and one in three.

I must study and struggle,
ride the seven seas and search the starry heavens.
I must gaze into my own heart
and devote myself to the ways of goodness.
I must sing until I am hoarse
and listen while I have ears to hear.

But in all this I still do not know
who you are.

I ask no more than this.

Jesus, I hear you say,
"Anyone who has seen me has seen God."

It is so. Amen.

Read: John 3.1-15

'You must all be born again.'

Pray for: The Congregational Federation

Birth

Warm Spirit of God,
sometimes we would like the security of our mother's womb,
to curl up in a safe corner of life
with no risks to take, no decisions to make for ourselves.
It is easy to stay in the places we know
and the habits we've got used to.
But now you call us to a new birth
with you, the Spirit, as our mother.

Spirit of God, let us be born anew.

Make us bold enough to be like children again.
Show us how to walk in ways that lead to justice.
Make us honest enough to tell you all our fears and failings.
Give us back the longing to touch and to kiss.
Treat us with devotion:
Hold us to your breast;
give us the confidence to risk ourselves;
and reassure us when we get hurt.

Spirit of God, let us be born anew.

We don't know where this new life will lead us
but we will let ourselves be carried along.
Let us take the chance of coming out into the light.
Through pain and blood,
through water and joy, we can be born again,
and whatever the way,
we know you will set us on the path to eternal life.

Spirit of God, let us be born anew.

Read: John 3.22-36

'This is my joy and now it is complete.'

Jesus said to his disciples, much later, that he had come to make their joy complete. Here, John the Baptist compares his feeling to that of the bridegroom's friend, whose joy is completed by the coming of the bridegroom, the fulfilment of the promise.

> Either imagine or discuss circumstances in which you might wish to say, 'Now my joy is complete.' As you discuss or imagine, let the sensation of joy arise from the instances mentioned. Let the joy spread through your mind, or in a group, watch it pass from person to person till it pervades the room.

Soweto Day
Pray for: The South Africa Council of Churches

Love casts out fear

I am afraid of the truth,
of my own wickedness,
my own lies and disasters and foolishness.

I am afraid of God,
with justice pure and fine,
who will not smile on compromise
or half-heartedness.

I am afraid of the prophet,
the angry man in the desert,
of words that burn my conscience
and shake the order of my ways.

I pray that the angry and fearful prophet
will grow less as Jesus grows more in me.
As the one from heaven
walks gently on the earth beside me,
I am less afraid.

There is truth and there are lies.
There is goodness and there is evil.
But there is also forgiveness and renewal.

As the fresh, flowing water of Jesus
restores me to life,
I will praise God for life in the desert,
for life in the city,
for life in me.

Read: John 4.5-26

'Sir', said the woman, 'give me this water, and then I shall not be thirsty, nor have to come all this way to draw water.'

Is it my imagination, or is the woman flirting with Jesus? After all, by the sound of it that is her customary way of relating to men. It is a common way for people to behave towards others who are of the opposite sex, just because they are. It is the approach of a woman who does not expect to be taken seriously.

She would, after all, not have been treated with courtesy or dignity by many of her own contemporaries, or, perhaps, by many of ours. She was a woman, and therefore to many a lesser human being. She had broken the standards of her own society, and was therefore an outcast.

In these circumstances, Jesus' responses are interesting. Not only does he treat her in all courtesy as another human being, but he allows her own innate intelligence to surface through the sophisticated defences she has built up for day to day living.

> Try reading the passage through with the idea of a flirtatious approach in mind, or, if you are in a group, read it as a dialogue. What does this do to the interaction, and to the serious and rather mysterious responses of Jesus?

Pray for: The United Church of Zambia

PRAYING WITH CWM CHURCHES 1996

Please use this leaflet as a part of your prayer life, individually or corporately, within a congregation. Suggestions for prayer can be supplemented and updated by using the Worship section of *News Share*, available from your church offices.

Africa

Presbyterian Church of Southern Africa (PCSA)

Give thanks for:

✦ Shirley and Murray Smith who work in Mozambique and Michelle Black, a Training In Mission student, that their faith may be deepened.

Pray that:

✦ Deeper involvement in the life and witness of CWM will continue;

✦ Spiritual and numerical growth will continue as the Church approaches its centenary in 1997.

Church of Jesus Christ in Madagascar (FJKM)

Give thanks for:

✦ The rehabilitation of some FJKM schools which have been damaged by cyclones or age, and the rehabilitation of the building of the Community of Sisters;

✦ The success of the theological training course for lay people.

Pray for the further training of lay pastors.

Madagascar: Women learn skills through programmes run by Dorkasy — the Women's Department of the Church of Jesus Christ in Madagascar

United Congregational Church of Southern Africa (UCCSA)

Give thanks that:

✦ The Church, with ecumenical partners, is in the forefront of efforts to bring about a just and democratically elected government in South Africa, Namibia and Mozambique;

✦ There is engagement in nation building and community development in these countries and Zimbabwe.

United Church of Zambia (UCZ)

Rejoice with the youth as they:

✦ Organise Bible studies and prayer meetings;

✦ Carry out visitation.

Give thanks and pray for:

✦ Lay training being carried out in the presbyteries as this provides alternative ministries to the expensive ordained ministry;

✦ Income generating projects to cut the cost of pastoral and social services.

Churches of Christ in Malawi (CCM)

Give thanks that:

✦ Women and youth are participating in the mission of the church.

Please pray for:

✦ The expansion and development of income generating projects;

✦ An improvement in communications;

✦ Leadership development.

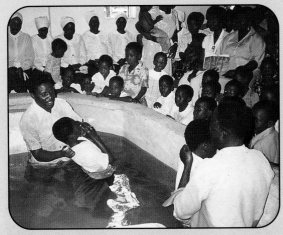

Malawi: Baptism at Zingwangwa Church, Blantyre

Europe

Congregational Federation (CF)

Give thanks for:

✦ The rich diversity of churches within the denomination;

✦ The many people attending leadership training courses;

✦ The youth coordinator who is carrying out a variety of work.

Pray for:

✦ The assimilation of over 30 Congregational churches into the life of the Federation;

✦ The four young people who visited Madagascar on an experience enlargement visit so that they may share faithfully the insights received.

United Reformed Church in the United Kingdom (URCUK)

Give thanks for mission achievements which include:

✦ A growing recognition in churches and society that the arms trade is unacceptable in its present, economically dominant form in the UK;

✦ The greater frequency of quiet days and retreats for members, elders and ministers;

✦ Growing theological agreement and closer working with other churches.

UK: Worship time at the CWM European Region Conference — Window on the World — held at Swanwick each summer

Reformed Churches in the Netherlands (RCN)

Give thanks for the vision of the Board for Mission and World Service as they encourage members to:

✦ Challenge each other in their congregations to be serving, missionary congregations of Christ in their own situations;

✦ Be open towards cooperation with non-christian organisations;

✦ Pursue peace and reconciliation especially in efforts to combat racism;

✦ And to reach the poor by mission and service.

Congregational Union of Scotland (CUS)

Pray that:

✦ The Youth in Mission perspective will be developed;

✦ Congregations will become sensitive to the meaning of mission in the community;

✦ Ecumenical mission projects will be sustained.

Presbyterian Church of Wales (PCW)

Rejoice in:

✦ The development of church community work, particularly at Noddfa, Caernarvon and Maesgeirchen, Bangor and pray that more community based ministries will be developed where appropriate;

✦ The signs of renewed interest in local mission in some congregations;

✦ The continuing development of chaplaincy work within industry and higher education.

Union of Welsh Independents (UWI)

Prayers are requested as plans are laid to call together all ministers in pastoral charge to consider the future ministry of the Union.

Pray that they will be enabled by God to discern his will for the work and witness of local congregations.

East Asia

Gereja Presbyterian Malaysia (PCM)

Rejoice that the Church is carrying out evangelism and church planting, some of which takes place in shops and houses.

Pray for christian teachers who are opting for early retirement to take up training as preachers.

Presbyterian Church in Singapore (PCS)

Pray for the continuing programmes of:

✦ Ministry to, and the building of homes for, the elderly;

✦ Heng Teck welfare centre which provides children's play and education facilities.

Rejoice that church growth and lay training are priorities.

Presbyterian Church of Korea (PCK)

Rejoice that the National Organisation of Korean Women:

✦ Supports schools and education;

✦ Organises a clinic for women on low incomes;

✦ Is involved in publishing and broadcasting.

Presbyterian Church of Myanmar (MPC)

Pray for priorities in:

✦ Leadership development, including training for the laity;

✦ Stewardship campaigns.

Rejoice that one-third of giving is spent on mission.

Pray for the work in the Baby Home for abandoned children.

Hong Kong Council of the Church of Christ in China (HKCCCC)

Pray for the Church as it seeks to:

✦ Promote and strengthen theological formation for the laity;

✦ Have closer links with the Church in China.

Pray with the church:

Grant us wisdom, grant us courage, for the facing of this hour
Grant us wisdom, grant us courage, for the living of these days.

Presbyterian Church in Taiwan (PCT)

Pray for the church's involvement in:

✦ The rebuilding of the spirituality of the people in Taiwan;

✦ Strengthening relations with the ecumenical community;

✦ A greater mobilisation, integration and sharing of resources;

✦ Increasing missionary personnel in response to the *Year 2000 Gospel Movement*.

Taiwan: The Presbyterian Church in Taiwan takes to the park for this children's event with music, drama and games

Pacific

Nauru Congregational Church (NCC)

Pray for:

✦ The plans to train church members for ministry;

✦ Attempts to train youth leaders through the Training in Mission scheme;

✦ The induction of two members to assist with pastoral work.

Congregational Christian Church in American Samoa (CCCAS)

Give thanks that the Church has been joyfully received as a partner within the CWM family. Pray that the leaders and members will be enabled to play a full role within the partnership and that they and other CWM partners will receive great benefit from CCCAS participation.

Kiribati Protestant Church (KPC)

Give thanks for:

✦ The successful establishment of secondary schools;

✦ The outreach programme in three southern islands where pastors, lay people and youth are encouraged.

Pray for the activities of the island church councils, village congregations and youth and women's groups as they reach remote communities with God's word.

Ekalesia Kelisiano Tuvalu (EKT)

Give thanks as the Church helps the nation by the provision of secondary education for underprivileged children who cannot get into a government school.

Pray for:

✦ The evangelical outpost to be established in the Outer Islands;

✦ The encouragement of mission with hospitals, prisons, expatriates and seamen.

Congregational Christian Church in Samoa (CCCS)

Give thanks for the personnel serving through CWM in various partner churches.

Pray for:

✦ The development of leadership training for young people;

✦ The leaders of the country, both in the church and government.

Congregational Union of New Zealand (CUNZ)

Give thanks for the Te Atatu Congregational Church which was received into full membership of the Union and for the appointment of a pastor.

Pray for the mission proposal to reach out to the various Pacific Island church groups and to encourage and help the people.

Presbyterian Church of Aotearoa New Zealand (PCANZ)

Give thanks for:

✦ The increasing sense of mission in the presbyteries;

✦ Effective evangelism in many congregations.

Pray for:

✦ The development of an understanding that the whole resources of the Church are for mission;

✦ The maintaining of an effective team of mission resource people in each presbytery.

United Church in Papua New Guinea and the Solomon Islands (UCPNGSI)

Give thanks for:

✦ The Women's Fellowship which is very active in local churches;

✦ Leadership training for children's workers and the ministry to children;

✦ The personnel from the Solomon Islands serving in the Highland Region and for the personnel from Papua New Guinea who serve the aborigines in Australia.

(Front cover – Papua New Guinea: Church thanksgiving)

South Asia

Presbyterian Church of India (PCI)

Give thanks for:

✦ The personnel who have been trained and sent out, within and outside the country;

✦ Houses which have been built for rural, disadvantaged refugees;

✦ The self employment programmes on basic engineering;

✦ The awareness seminars for the rights of women for ordination into the full-time ministry.

Church of Bangladesh (CoB)

Pray for:

✦ The priority of spiritual and social development of all people;

✦ The importance of relating faith and work in all church programmes;

✦ The presbyters and that the need for more will be met;

✦ The establishment of in-service training for teachers.

Bangladesh: One of the ways the Ratanpur Agricultural Service Centre helps poor families is by thatching their homes

Church of South India (CSI)

Give thanks for the Women's Fellowship and their:

✦ Sponsored leadership training programmes;

✦ Retreats for working women;

✦ Prayer workshops;

✦ Commitment to marriage and family life education.

Church of North India (CNI)

Rejoice in the implementation of the holistic understanding of mission throughout the church at congregational level.

Please continue to pray for:

✦ Holistic mission efforts;

✦ Meaningful involvement in the lives of people for the Justice, Peace and Integrity of Creation programme.

I Dare to Dream

I dare to dream
No more people die of starvation
I dare to dream
No more people die of diseases
I dare to dream
People no longer kill one another
I dare to dream
People live in peace and harmony
I dare to dream
Justice, peace and love prevail over all
I dare to dream
Because God Our Lord is alive
And He loves and cares for us
He is Our Heavenly Father
And we are His dearest children
Dare to dream
You people of God

(Church of Jesus Christ in Madagascar)

Continue to dream... Continue to hope... in the spirit of this prayer from the Church of Jesus Christ in Madagascar. Make your own prayers and meditations for each of our partners especially gathering thoughts from the pictures in this leaflet, eg, Pray that families will be given homes through the Ratanpur Agricultural Service Centre in Bangladesh; and pray for the work of FJKM through Dorkasy's programmes.

Caribbean

Guyana Congregational Union (GCU)

Pray that:

✦ There will be more candidates trained as ordained pastors;

✦ There will be continual involvement in the schools geared toward helping the disadvantaged in Guyanese society.

Give thanks for the Guyana Congregational Young People's Union as it conducts programmes of prayer and bible study, youth leadership development and the building of ecumenical links through projects such as the recent Youth in Mission Workcamp.

United Church in Jamaica and the Cayman Islands (UCJCI)

Give thanks for:

✦ The establishment of three new congregations;

✦ The tremendous inroads in youth ministry by young ministers in each council;

✦ The ministry to children through the two children's homes;

✦ The effective radio ministry on two radio stations.

Pray for the church's theme for the next two years, *Surely, Goodness and Mercy,* which aims at refocussing the two nations on the celebration of all that is good.

Jamaica: School children

Council for World Mission, Livingstone House,
11 Carteret Street, London SW1H 9DL, UK
Registered Charity No 232868
Printed by C H Healey Printers & Stationers, Ipswich IP4 1JL

Sharing the cup

Lord, we like to know where we stand,
who we are and where we belong.
Even our friends are carefully defined:
so our neat lives are not disturbed
by those we think too good for us
or those we think too bad.
We even know our class,
and find our conversation strained when we have to step outside it.

We build chapels where we can feel sure of you
and where walls can protect us.
We want to know we are your friends,
and we want others to think like us and believe like us,
or else to keep apart from us.
We set ourselves about with rules
to make us feel secure.
Things have to be done just so, or we get annoyed.
It feels good to know what's right and what's not.

So you trouble our shaky security
when you behave as if there were no rules
or as if they didn't matter.
You drink and chat with the woman
whom others would have despised,
and you shame our meagre hospitality.
You offer your best gifts to people we wouldn't even speak to -
if we didn't have to.

Your love takes us further than our rules allow.
You lead us on,
through chance meetings and casual relationships
which we might have despised
to find such satisfaction in love which knows no bounds.

Lord forgive us for our narrowness.
Let us welcome your love, for others, as for ourselves,
so we can unlock our hearts and demolish our sham walls
and welcome the gift of life.

Read: John 4.27-42

'The reaper is drawing his pay and harvesting a crop for eternal life so that sower and reaper may rejoice together.'

Jesus often talks of the harvest as an image for the work that is to be done. It is an image which carries with it the sense of present readiness after a time of waiting, while the seeds which have been sown grow to maturity. Now they are ready, and the harvest can begin. Here, the sowers of the seed join the harvesters in the festival.

It is as if his theological conversation with the woman at the well has given to Jesus the sense of years of preparation, years of quiet growth, waiting for the harvest, which is now about to be gathered in.

Her words were full of historic reference drawn from the long history of her people. The well is Jacob's well, father of Israel. The division between Judea and Samaria has its roots not only in a difference in worship, but in the long tribal and political past of the People of God.

Her story is part of her people's story: the seeds have been sown over generations. And at the time of harvest, when sowers and reapers get together, the generations join in the great celebration of all time.

Pray for:
The Hong Kong Council of the Church of Christ in China

Generous love

God, give us grace.

Give us the grace to celebrate the happiness of others,
to be pleased when others are glad,
to smile when others are surprised by love.

God, give us grace.

Give us the grace to be welcoming to anyone you give to us,
to greet others with open generosity,
to nurse no bitter reproaches or resentments.

God, give us grace.

Give us the grace to let even justice be overwhelmed by love,
to accept repentance without cynicism,
to be glad when there is no revenge.

God, give us grace.

Give us the grace to smile with ease,
even when we feel upstaged.
Give us the maturity to ride the day
when we do not get the credit we deserve.
Give the reassurance of your love
when we look for security in status or recognition.

God, give us grace.

Lord, give your grace to fragile and tender people
so that we will learn to love as you love,
with warmth, openness and graciousness.

God, give us grace. Amen.

Read: John 4.43-54

Jesus said, 'Will none of you ever believe without seeing signs and portents?'

Very often in John's gospel, Jesus reacts harshly to being asked to perform a miracle. Sometimes, as here, it seems unjustified. This official is not asking for proof of Jesus' authenticity. His motive is far more straightforward.

It is almost as if Jesus has an ambivalent attitude to his own miracles. They are signs, and bring people to belief. In fact, later in his ministry, he calls them as witnesses to his truth: 'If my deeds are not the deeds of my Father, do not believe me. But if they are, then even if you do not believe me, believe the deeds, so that you may recognize and know that the Father is in me, and I in the Father.' (10.37-38).

But he much prefers belief which is not dependent on seeing: which is a much tougher proposition. Thomas, who will not believe without seeing with his own eyes, and touching with his own hands, is told, 'Because you have seen me, you have found faith. Happy are those who find faith without seeing me.' (John 20.29)

Pray for: The Presbyterian Church in Singapore

Signs and wonders

God, sometimes we long for you to do something dramatic.
We have tried to be faithful and do what you've asked of us,
so would it be too much to do one small thing to prove us right
and show our faith has not been mistaken?
We have believed in you,
and it would be nice if others could see we were right all along.

Maybe tonight you could rearrange the stars
to spell out your glory more clearly.
But if not for us, then maybe you could do it for others,
so they too will believe.
Or could you show you are there by answering a few of our prayers?
World peace would be good for a start
and then an end to hunger.

Lord, when we get to thinking like this,
remind us of the signs of your love:
      where there is healing;
      where women and men give their lives for others;
      wherever death is defeated.

Even while we beg you
to heal those we love,
keep our eyes not on the signs and wonders
but on the fearful glory of your cross,
where what to the world seemed loss
was our gain.

Crucified Lord,
we praise you for the real sign and wonder of your love.

Read: John 5.19-36

'The time is coming when all who are in the grave shall hear his voice
and come out: those who have done right will rise to life; those who
have done wrong will rise to judgment.'

We are used to the idea of a Judgment from Matthew's gospel:
the sheep and goats, or the wise and foolish virgins. Armageddon
appears in Matthew, Mark and Luke, sometimes in terrifying
detail. Previously in this gospel, however, the judgment has been
more concerned with choices in this life: coming to the light, or
preferring the darkness (3.19-21). We judge ourselves by our
response to Jesus, the light.

Now, however, Jesus talks openly of a traditional judgment scene,
with the figure of the Son of Man, who, in Daniel's apocalyptic
writing, is representative of God's saints, bringing about the last
judgment which follows the resurrection of the dead. The language
is clear. Everyone will face judgment on his life or her life. Dying is
no escape.

However, Jesus is not only the mighty one whose voice calls the
dead from their graves to judgment. He is also, at least in the
minds of the Pharisees, the one who must stand trial. From this
time, the conversations with the Pharisees take on the language
of a trial, a judgment scene, with Jesus not as the judge, but the
accused.

Pray for: The Church of North India

Death is for real

They dream of immortality
and pretend death is nothing,
merely a door into the next room
where life continues.

But, God, now I understand that we are not immortal.
Death is something after all.
It has taken people I love
and grief makes me afraid.
It is turning my hair grey and is already emptying my memory.
I watch, helpless and terrified,
as it steals breath from hungry children
and as it ends at a single stroke the tenderly nurtured life
of a mother's son with a weapon in his hand.
We are not immortal.
We are mortal creatures,
spun of flesh and bone, of blood and tears.
Immortality is but the dream of those who cannot live
and who bear the dread of death.

I do not choose the empty hope of immortality,
the meagre, facile dream of a death which has no power.
I choose instead the miracle of resurrection,
which only you,
overturning the powers of decay and sorrow,
could work in us.
Only you could defeat the terrible enemy of us all,
could conquer that which is something,
and lead us,
not into the next room,
but into a new and unimagined life.

I pray, God, that you will give me and all people
life beyond death,
now and ever after,
so that I may face death and live.

Read: John 6.16-21

'It is I: do not be afraid.'

This might take its place as the least known of the famous 'I am'
sayings of Jesus recorded in John's gospel. Elsewhere, he says,
'I am the bread of life', 'I am the true vine', and so on. Here, he just
says, 'I am', though most translations have something like, 'It is I',
which makes more sense in the context.

It is impossible to know what the original words of Jesus were,
since they would have been spoken in Aramaic, but when John
translates them into Greek, he makes it quite clear that we are to
understand something of great significance. The only bearer of
the name 'I AM', the name too holy to be spoken, is God. This is
the name revealed to Moses from the burning bush (Exodus 3.14).
Jesus' implied use of the divine name is elsewhere considered to
be blasphemy by the Jewish authorities.

But here, in the desperate chaos of the sudden storm, with the
real danger of drowning, the disciples are to be reassured simply
because Jesus is.

Similarly, in the desperate chaos of the sudden storms that beset
our lives, we are to be reassured because Jesus is, and because his
being reflects the being which is at the heart of God. The promise
of God is not that the storm will be stilled - that belongs to another
story, and does not happen here - but that God's awesome presence
is with us in the storm, walking towards us over the very waves
which threaten to engulf us. The story reflects the promise in
Isaiah 43, 'When you pass through water I shall be with you;
when you pass through rivers they will not overwhelm you.'
(Isaiah 43.2)

Pray for: The Church of Bangladesh

Isaiah 43.1-13;
Acts 27.33-44;
John 6.16-21

Pe... 28 Ju...

Do not be afraid

Knowing that Jesus is present
in the fury and turmoil that frighten us,
let us pray for ourselves and for all who are afraid.

For those who fear that they cannot cope,
whose lives seem to collapse about them,
who reckon that they are failures
or consider suicide.
To them, God says:
Do not fear, I am with you.

For those who worry for others,
who are anxious for a friend or relative who is ill, or dying,
or for a child or parent who needs more care than we can find.
To them, God says:
Do not fear, I am with you.

For those trapped by catastrophe or war,
deprived of their homes,
separated from family, dependent on charity,
without work or wealth.
To them, God says:
Do not fear, I am with you.

For someone who sleeps rough tonight,
for a woman caught in violence at home,
for a child who cannot tell
about the torment and indignity she faces,
for those who will not sleep because the dark contains terrors
which they dare not name.
To them, God says:
Do not fear, I am with you.

And for ourselves, as we name and face our own fears,
maybe thinking they threaten to engulf us.
To us, God says:
**Do not fear, I am with you.
It is I; do not be afraid.**

Read: John 6.22-27

'In very truth I tell you it is not because you saw signs that you came looking for me, but because you ate the bread and your hunger was satisfied.'

John's gospel is always working at two levels. Perfectly ordinary things are invested with extraordinary significance. Even extraordinary events are not simply what they seem. Water turns to wine, the dead are raised to life, a hungry crowd is fed. But all this is not simply so that wedding guests can celebrate or people's hunger may be allayed, or even to restore their brother to his friends.

The word, 'sign' is a hint. The miracles concentrate the mind on ordinary things: bread which fills you up and stops you feeling hungry and keeps you alive; wine which makes the party go with a swing and without which a celebration is a disaster; the comfortable presence of a loved member of the family, whose loss is an inconsolable grief.

Then the ordinary becomes the gateway to a new insight. What really gives life - eternal life? What food endures so that the eater will not be hungry again? The crowd missed the point of the miracle, and came back for more.

Once they began to understand, of course, they stopped coming back.

Pray for: The Guyana Congregational Union

The food of love

We praise you God for the taste of the Kingdom
in eating and drinking,
for the pleasures of taste and smell,
of a full stomach and of tipsy forgetfulness.
For soup and savour, for sweet and sour,
for deep, red wine and fresh, whipped cream, we praise you.
From the fleshly delights of food and drink,
from satisfaction, from the pleasant anticipation of hunger,
we know your Kingdom as feast and fellowship, and we are glad.

We pray for those who do not taste heaven in eating and drinking.
We pray for those who are hungry,
who long for flour to bake bread
and oil to make skin shine with health.
We pray for those who take little pleasure
in their meagre rations or their boring diet.
We pray for all who eat only prison food
and who long for some favourite meal prepared with love.

We pray for those who are afraid of food,
who live in terror of allergy or poison.
We pray for those who believe they are too fat,
but whose bodies are slimming to nothing by dieting or purging.

We pray for all who do not taste the Kingdom of heaven
in eating and drinking,
for whom food is a dream or a nightmare.

And as food is shared among us,
in our homes, in cafés or restaurants,
in a picnic in the park or a business lunch,
in a fellowship supper or in holy communion,
let us pray that its calories and its context,
will give us all strength
to live for one another and for God,
so that, one day, all God's children may be fed
and taste at last the food of eternal life.

Read: John 6.41-59

'Whoever eats my flesh and drinks my blood has eternal life, and I will raise him up on the last day.'

Here is a table that is round, that is round,
And strong are its timbers, wide its bound'ries.
Better artistry cannot be found, not be found,
And we are that table that is round.

And on that table there is bread, there is bread
Made of spices for healing, grains nature-fed.
The ingredients lovingly prepared, prepared,
And we are that nourishing loaf of bread.

And on that table there is wine, there is wine,
Apple cider and champagne, Russian vodka,
For the earth gives the finest of the fine for to dine,
And we are that finest, we are new wine.

And round that table there are hands holding hands,
And the fingers touch fingers, palms clasp palms,
And they stretch across the ocean, cross the lands, cross the lands,
And we are those fingers, we are hands.

© *Betty Wendelborn (1939-)*
Used by permission

(Music for these words can be found at back of book)

Pray for:
The Presbyterian Church of Aotearoa New Zealand

Whoever eats my flesh

Sometimes, God, I'm tempted to think I have all I need.
A freezer stocked with enough to see out a famine,
a feast of entertainment in my own living room.
It takes words like these to remind me
that even when I've had my tea
I'm still hungry.
Forgive me when I've skimmed over them.
Forgive me when I've dismissed them as crude
because they sound too much like cannibalism.
I need their directness to wake me
and stop me thinking I can get all I need without you.

Maybe I've been persuaded for too long
that what the ads say is true;
that if I had just one more thing,
a new car, whiter washing, a better pension,
I could be happy.
But you say that there is no satisfaction apart from you.
And when I want to curl up on my own,
you call me out and you say again and again:
I am the bread of life,
　　　eat this bread
　　　eat my flesh.

So let me taste you in the fellowship of your people.
Let me enjoy your presence at your own table
and let me discover that the deep hunger I feel
can be met by you:
　　　when I long for the wisdom to see what is right,
　　　and then to do it;
　　　when I see how all my other cravings lead me nowhere;
　　　when I meet people in desperate need, crying children,
　　　friends who cannot see the way through their problems;
　　　when life tastes sour and all my greed cannot make it sweet;
then let me eat the bread that all can share,
and taste the life that death cannot destroy.
My hunger is deep, God.
I hope you can fill it.

Read: John 7.1-17

'He is a good man,' said some. 'No,' said others, 'he is leading people astray.'

At the centre of John's gospel lies the great debate. Was Jesus to be believed or not? The gospel does its best to convince, promising eternal life to those who believe (3.16) and offering the personal testimony of the writer (19.35). But it does not shirk the other side of the debate, put by the Pharisees and the people.

> If you do this exercise, alone or in a group, do so with great sensitivity and care.
>
> Divide the congregation or group into two halves, or engage in your own inner debate. One side will argue for believing in Jesus, and the other will argue against. Each side can use the gospel record, but also the record of Christian believers through the ages. Believing in Jesus has been tried for 2,000 years. Has it succeeded, or failed? What are the criteria on which success and failure are judged?
>
> Either side may like to use personal experience, as does the gospel writer. What is the value of personal testimony?
>
> This is the great debate. Everything hangs on this. Is the gospel true and valid, or is it simply leading people astray? What are you going to do if the noes have it?
>
> This exercise must end in an act of pastoral care, for those who have questioned their faith perhaps for the first time, or more deeply than before.

This is not an imaginary exercise, of course, since the great debate goes on in people's lives every day.

Pray for: Christians in Public Life
Westhill College, Selly Oak, Birmingham B29 6LL

True tales

A youth group meets in a basement, sharing faith over coffee,
flirting with each other and with God,
testing the truth, looking for love and wisdom.

The women meet in the afternoon for fellowship and bingo,
for laughter and a tear and a little forgetting
of whatever pain they bear.
They dare, now and again, to say something so true
that they think the minister would be appalled.

The Boys Brigade assemble for drill and games
and a quiet one whispers to the chaplain
of his dead sister and says it's terrible.

The members gather with long agenda and tired faces,
bearing up the weight of their task.
And in the Bible Study someone jokes
and the lightness of truth makes trouble easier.

An ordinand sheds tears over an essay
that she cannot mean, but must be written
and a prayer that she does mean, but how to say it?

A child speaks wisdom in answer to the preacher's question,
but everyone laughs at such small talk.

How is it that these people have such learning,
when they have never been taught?

Thank God for truth tellers and their tales.

Read: John 7.40-52

Have you been taken in too?

REASONS FOR NOT BELIEVING:

a)   He doesn't have the right pedigree - his accent's all wrong -
      he's got the wrong parents - people like us don't believe in
      people like him.

b)   It doesn't accord with the Bible. Either you believe in the Bible
      or you don't, and if you do, you don't have to believe this.

c)   No-one else believes - maybe he's convinced a few uneducated
      yobbos and women and that, but no-one real.

And last, and very important:

d)   Give any dog who sticks with him the same bad name -
      'You must be one of them.' (i.e. not one of us).

This list of excuses will fit almost any awkward situation the
self-respecting Christian may encounter. Equipped with these,
you will be able to avoid joining any good cause, siding with
anyone, or generally having to take any action at all.

Pray for: The Presbyterian Church of Korea

Believing

Jesus,
following you does not always make us popular.
In Ordsall and Sparkbrook,
from Welsh valleys to Scottish islands,
the crowds do not go after you
as once they did.
Yet as it was in Jerusalem, so it is today,
your voice is still heard amongst us.

> **For God's foolishness is wiser than human wisdom
> and God's weakness is stronger than human strength.**

Show us where prophets speak today,
in places as unlikely as Galilee:
in the Salems and Bethels and Ebenezers
where you are still praised;
on street corners, and on the doorstep
where the Gospel is still shared;
in the political meeting and the prayer meeting
as good news is spread,
the marginal are given pride of place,
and the Messiah is amongst us again.

> **For God's foolishness is wiser than human wisdom
> and God's weakness is stronger than human strength.**

Give us the faith,
not to succumb to the merely popular,
but to stay with you
when no one listens and our beliefs are ridiculed.
Give us the words to say,
when others think we look foolish,
when they wonder how we were taken in
by such a strange Messiah.

> **For God's foolishness is wiser than human wisdom
> and God's weakness is stronger than human strength.**

Read: John 8. 3-11

Making her stand in the middle, they said to him, 'Teacher, this woman was caught in the very act of adultery.'

The following words were written on tear-shaped pieces of paper at a service for survivors of sexual abuse.

'I weep as a relative of an abused person, unable to appease or comfort the torment caused by the abuser. I weep with anger at my inadequacy'

'I weep for all those children who think the abuse is their fault.'

'I weep for the way in which my abuse has ruined every relationship I've ever had.'

'I weep for my mum who was too frightened to stop her father abusing me.'

'I weep for the loss of joy, hope, security, creativity, confidence, for the loss of my child in a sea of fear and insecurity - the abuse of self.'

'I weep for children who are abused by clergy and ministers . . . for children who are abused inside our Christian homes and communities . . .'

'I weep for all who are broken in spirit, because of the acts of others.'

Pray for: CSSA (Christian Survivors of Sexual Abuse)
London WC1N 3XX

God loves a woman

**The stones remain on the earth,
for the heart of God is warm towards all that God has made.**

We are the scribes and pharisees,
so eager to condemn a woman's sin,
relishing the sharp stones, the tablets of the law.
We know the pleasure of judgement
and the power of righteousness.

**The stones remain on the earth,
for the heart of God is warm towards all that God has made.**

We are the woman,
the secret sin at last revealed,
the one thing we had risked
for joy and the banishment of loneliness.
We know the terror of condemnation.

**The stones remain on the earth,
for the heart of God is warm towards all that God has made.**

We are the woman's lover,
fled from the consequences
or set free by unjust custom.
We know the temptation to hide from the truth.

**The stones remain on the earth,
for the heart of God is warm towards all that God has made.**

We see Jesus,
who knew the power and passion of the body,
who suffered the taunts and hatred of a mob,
silent before his accusers and innocent of all guilt,
yet despised and shamed.
We see Jesus who rose from the stones.

**The stones remain on the earth,
for the heart of God is warm towards all that God has made.**

Jesus says to us:
"I do not condemn you. Go your way, and do not sin again."

Read: John 8.12-20

My testimony is valid

What is God's testimony like? The following is taken from John McCarthy and Jill Morell's book, *Some Other Rainbow*. It is John's account of events near the beginning of his five years as a hostage in Beirut.

'I was to be in this solitary cell for less than three months, but after the first two to three weeks it felt as if I had slipped into a different time-scale. Days passed without any variation. The food-and-bathroom run and then nothing. I read and re-read everything available. I relived much of my life and made endless plans for the future. But after two months with not the slightest hint that I might be released I got more frightened. So many of my reflections had left me feeling inadequate that I began to doubt that I could cope alone.

'One morning these fears became unbearable. I stood in the cell sinking into despair. I felt that I was literally sinking, being sucked down into a whirlpool. I was on my knees, gasping for air, drowning in hopelessness and helplessness. I thought that I was passing out. I could only think of one thing to say - "Help me please, oh God, help me." The next instant I was standing up, surrounded by a warm bright light. I was dancing, full of joy. In the space of a minute, despair had vanished, replaced by boundless optimism.

'What had happened? I had never had any great faith, despite a Church of England upbringing. But I felt that I had to give thanks. But to what? Unsure of the nature of the experience, I felt most comfortable acknowledging the Good Spirit which seemed to have rescued me.

'It gave me great strength to carry on and, more importantly, a huge renewal of hope - I was going to survive. Throughout my captivity, I would take comfort from this experience, drawing on it whenever optimism or determination flagged.'

Extract from "Some Other Rainbow"
by John McCarthy and Jill Morrell. Reproduced by permission.

Pray for: The Church of Jesus Christ in Madagascar

Testimony

Pray this week for those who testify to the light of the world.

Pray for those who testify by sharing their faith:
who placard the good news;
or preach from the pulpit;
or pass on their faith in quiet conversation.

Pray for those who testify by their lives
to what they believe in their hearts:
who give away their possessions;
who share resources, living simply for the sake of others;
who will not cease to work to give justice
    for those wrongly imprisoned
    or harshly treated by the state.

Pray for those put on trial for living their faith.

Pray for those who help us to testify:
who share in CWM's education in mission programme;
who help churches to witness to the gospel of Christ;
and pray for all who have shared their faith with you
    or given you the courage and the confidence
    to share your own faith.

Finally, pray for your own testimony,
that it will be valid,
that it will point to Christ,
that it will reach others,
so that they too may know Jesus
and the Father also.

In a group, sing as a round, to the tune Frere Jacques:

Wake up, sleeper! Wake up, sleeper!
Rise from the dead! Rise from the dead!
Christ will shine upon you. Christ will shine upon you.
You are light. You are light.

Ephesians 5:14,8
para. Charles Robertson (1940-)

Read: John 8.(31-36) 37-47

' . . . because I speak the truth, you do not believe me.'

The devil's bastards, Jesus calls them - or that is how they respond - 'We are not illegitimate,' literally, 'We are not born of fornication.' Who? The Jews who had believed! These were supposedly the people who were on Jesus' side, and still they wanted to pull rank and ensure that there were outsiders.

Who are the devil's bastards today? We can't look for them outside our own circle, for they are the ones who are supposedly on the inside. They are believers. They claim true descent and access to divine privilege, and they hide their false parentage even from themselves.

Perhaps we ought to change the 'them' to 'us', for as soon as we find the truth too hard to bear and start trying to ensure that we are in, and others are out, Satan smiles as he welcomes us to his inner circle.

Racial Justice Sunday
Pray for: CCRJ (the Churches Commission on Racial Justice)
Interchurch House, 35-41 Lower Marsh, London SE1 7RL.

All children of God's love

God save us!

We pray for those who are cast out because of their race,
named 'outsider', 'bastard' and worse.
We remember the ovens of the death camps,
the swastikas on smashed graves,
the slogans in the underpass.
We have heard the street taunts,
the playground bullying,
and the jokes at their expense.

God save us!

We pray for those who are racist,
finding and using an illegitimate power.
We remember the skinheads and the nicely suited politicians,
the fascists and the frightened ones.
We have heard the racism of the far-right
and the nice racism of the suburbs.
We have known it in ourselves,
born from fear and pride and ignorance.

God save us!

We pray that you will take away our fear,
whoever we are and wherever we stand.
Show us that we are yours,
your children born from grace and love.
Save us from our jealousies and hatreds,
and make us look with love into the faces
of our brothers and sisters,
who are, with us, your children.

God save us!

Read: John 10.1-6

'They will not follow a stranger; they will run away from him, because they do not recognise his voice'

The Island of Yell is the middle of the three main Shetland Islands, and parts of it are extremely remote. The sheep and lambs which graze the bogs and the headlands have a difficult life. Many lambs die and become carrion. In late May and early June, there are lots of little empty carcasses.

Of course the standard of shepherding is very high, and generally, even on their own, the ewes are very protective. They can be heard constantly calling to their lambs, making sure they are safe. If you disturb a lamb, it will run towards its mother's call, but a lamb on its own is vulnerable.

One day, while walking on the West coast of this remote island, cut off by miles of peat bog from any other person, we heard the familiar bleating of a lamb. But there was no answering call. The lamb kept on bleating, and, instead of running away from us, came towards us, and stood, gazing at us and bleating, heart-breakingly.

We could do nothing. There was no shepherd for three or four hours' walking distance. If we picked up the lamb, which every instinct in us wanted to do, we might have removed it from its only real safety, the missing ewe.

So we walked on. And the bleating followed us for half an hour or so. There was no shepherd, no ewe, no familiar voice, no safety.

The analogy is not exact, since our Shepherd is not remote or unavailable. But, failing to hear his voice, people will turn to us or to anyone, seeking what only the Shepherd can give.

Pray for: The Congregational Christian Church in Samoa

Calling of voices

Lord,
so many voices call to us.
Not all of them are yours.
Make us careful to hear your own firm voice
        and to know it from the great blaring voice
        of our mass culture.

We hear brash voices telling us
        that what matters about work is the size of the salary,
        that what matters about life is the status we achieve.
And you gently call to us,
"This way, follow me."

Like lost sheep,
we are tempted to follow any voice we hear,
hoping we will be led to safety.
Yet when we hear your voice we want no other shepherd.

So, call to us,
in the gentle voices of compassion
and the angry voices of protest.

Call to us,
in the screams of a child
and the tenderness of an embrace.

Call to us,
through the fears which keep us awake
and in the rest which soothes our anxiety.

Call to us,
in the excitement of love
and in the freedom of trust.

Lord, call to us,
and we will know your voice,
and we will follow you.

Read: John 10. 22-30

' . . .*because you are not sheep of my flock, you do not believe. My own sheep listen to my voice; I know them and they follow me. I give them eternal life and they will never perish. No-one can snatch them out of the Father's care.*'

How do you become part of the flock?

It seems that, once you are in, the benefits are clear. You hear and understand the voice of the shepherd; you have someone to follow; you are given eternal life and you are safe. Yet, if you are not one of the flock, none of this is available - most notably, understanding the voice of Jesus, who seems to be the only way in.

If you cannot get in without hearing Jesus, and you cannot hear Jesus unless you are in, what hope is there? Isaiah knew something of this, in his words, quoted by Jesus, 'However hard you listen you will never understand. However hard you look, you will never see.' (Isaiah 6.8).

And yet, there *must* be a way to change from not being part of the flock to being part of it. You can't be *born* in or out. The question is not negligible. The possibility of real change, repentance and rebirth is at the heart of the charge to evangelise.

The gospel story is full of people who did come to believe, and this step of faith is the declared purpose of John's gospel (John 20.31).

Pray for: CCOM (the Churches Commission on Mission)
Interchurch House, 35-41 Lower Marsh, London SE1 7RL.

You spoke first

Gentle Lord,
as I remember my days,
I thank you for all that has made me who I am.
My genes -
   did you know that my mother and my father would make - me?
My childhood, its bliss and its agony -
   did you plan it that way
   so that I would be like this?
All the things I have learned from books and people,
of what is holy and what is profane -
   was it you teaching me and guiding me?
All the things I have chosen,
people to love, work to do, pleasure and pain -
   were they my choosing or yours?

I can tell it both ways.
I know there were things I chose carefully,
moments when I seized the moment and made a choice -
   for her, for him, for you.
And I know that I did not choose,
that I could not have done it differently,
that I was chosen.

I have to tell it both ways.
Both make sense.
I choose and I am chosen.

Gentle Lord,
sweet shepherd,
I listen for your voice
but you spoke first.

Read: John 10. 31-42

'. . . *the Father is in me, and I in the Father.*'

Pray for: The Union of Welsh Independents

Claiming to be God

God,
I want no sham messiah,
with empty claims,
untouched by human life.

I have to know
that you are not afraid to face my fears:
you see the way I want to hide
and you choose to share the dark with me.

I have to know
that you feel my pain:
you sense the hurt that lies within
and you cry for me and hold me to your cheek.

I have to know
that you share my joy:
you know the pleasures that love can bring
and you come and celebrate with me.

I have to know
that you hold me close:
you feel the warmth of intimacy
and you live in those I love.

I have to know
that you are not remote,
returned to heaven, enthroned on high
but with me now in whatever I do.

I have to know
that you are God:
I have to know that you are like me,
a man, a woman, a child.

Read: John 11.1-16

Thomas, called 'the Twin', said to his fellow disciples, 'Let us go and die with him.'

Lazarus is dead. 'Let us,' says Thomas, 'go and die', for if Jesus takes the course of utmost folly and goes to see Lazarus' family, soon they'll all be dead. Even Jesus talks of nightfall.

And surely the night is drawing in. Jesus, like the Priest at the end of Graham Greene's novel, *The Power and the Glory*, like countless heroes before and since, turns his face and goes back, towards the danger, the end, which is his destiny.

If this were simply a rattling good story, some good would come of his courageous act. Jesus would escape dramatically from death, or he and the others might be swept into the night, but there would be a new dawn, new disciples, a realisation (alas too late) that he'd been right all along.

But this is no romantic tragedy. What happens is beyond the bounds of a good story. There is no fairy tale ending, but rather the salvation of the world.

Caiaphas recognises the importance of this moment. He says to the Pharisees, 'You have no grasp of the situation at all; you do not realize that it is more to your interest that one man should die for the people than that the whole nation should be destroyed.' (John 11.49b-50)

From this point on the debate has ended and the battle is finally joined.

Pray for: Ekalesia Kelisiano Tuvalu

For the love of Jesus

Light a candle for each witness remembered.

Let us remember in quietness all who have died with Jesus,
those who have faced the darkness
and, out of conscience, stubbornness or terror,
gone to their death for their faith.

> Stephen
> Peter
> Sebastian
> Perpetua and Felicity
> Anne Askew
> Thomas Cranmer
> John Penry
> Eric Liddell
> Alfred Sadd
> Diane Thompson and Sharon Swindells
> Martin Luther King
> and many others ...

Name those you wish to recall.

God, give us courage to face the great pain
of the world's indifference.
For us, there is no grand tragedy,
but a terrible and savage comedy
as the world finds us amusing and strange.

Let us also go and die with Jesus,
and hold us firm
so that we do not stumble
in the daylight's glare
or perish in the dark of night.
May we turn our faces to the terrors of our own age
and, with wisdom and bravery, walk with our Lord.

Light a candle to represent your own witness to Christ.

Read: John 11.28-44

Jesus said, 'I am the resurrection and the life. Whoever believes in me shall live, even though he dies, and no-one who lives and has faith in me shall ever die. Do you believe this?'

Pray for:
The Nauru
Congregational
Church

Life and death

God, when I hear the news today,
there is little encouragement to believe in stories of risen bodies.
A child, not even known by name, lies unburied at a roadside.
In wreckage and disaster, someone's brother, someone's sister,
is dead before rescue can arrive.

God, why weren't you there?
Is your spirit not troubled by what you see?
Cannot you take the stone away for me,
from graves already cold
and put your glory
where now there's just a stench?

I know that sometimes there is hope;
those thought already dead are found still living,
but that's not resurrection.

I want to believe, that even where I cannot see,
and when the tomb stays sealed,
resurrection is just as true.

Yet this I know:
Whatever happens with the bones,
you are the resurrection and the life.

So when I believe, when I want to believe,
and when belief is hard for me,
help me to confess:
"Yes, Lord, I believe that you are the Messiah,
the Son of God,
the one coming into the world."

You are the resurrection and the life.

Read: John 17.13-26

'May they all be one; as you, Father, are in me and I in you so may they be in us, that the world may believe that you sent me.'

A wedding couple choose their rings. They choose rings made of three types of gold, wound together into one ring. During the ceremony, they place the rings on each other's fingers. The ring wraps the finger round, three strands of pure gold wound together, a sign and symbol for all the world to see.

And by the one ring made of three woven strands of gold, one on each hand, the bride and groom proclaim and celebrate two becoming one, the fulfilment of creation: 'That is why a man leaves his father and mother and attaches himself to his wife, and the two become one.' (Genesis 2.7)

This, in turn, mirrors a greater mystery. God, too, is one and more than one, and this is woven into our imaging of God. Note the way in which singular and plural are interwoven in the account of our creation. 'Then God said, 'Let us make human being in our own image, after our likeness" . . . God created human being in his image; in the image of God he created them; male and female he created them.' (Genesis 1.26-27. I have translated 'Adam', 'human being', reflecting the fact that it is singular in the original language).

God is one and three.
We are many and one.
This is the mystery.
Alleluia.

One World Week
Pray for: The World Development Movement
25 Beehive Place, London SW9 7QR

One in love

Praise God for love!
- for love which turns us to one another
to look with surprise into the eyes of a different face
and to see one who belongs to us.

Praise God for love!
- for love which draws us together,
out of strangeness and indifference,
to find friendship and union.

Praise God for love!
- for love which touches us from God,
reaching across the divide, defying the distance,
bringing us close, uniting us to God.

Praise God for love!
In love with each other,
in love with God,
in the love of God,
we belong.

Praise God!

Read: John 1.1-14

In the beginning the Word already was. The Word was in God's presence, and what God was, the Word was.

'In God's presence' is a very interesting translation. It brings out a parallel between this passage and the lovely poem of creation at Proverbs 8.22-30, where God and Wisdom are first mother and daughter, then playmates, then a design team. God gives birth to Wisdom at the beginning of creation.

> *The LORD created me the first of his works*
> *long ago before all else that he made*
> *I was formed in earliest times,*
> *at the beginning, before earth itself.*
> *I was born when there was yet no ocean,*
> *when there were no springs brimming with water.*

Wisdom was in God's presence at the beginning of all things, a constant delight, giving pleasure to God and taking pleasure in the world, and especially in humankind.

> *Then I was at his side each day,*
> *his darling and delight,*
> *playing in his presence continually,*
> *playing over the whole world,*
> *while my delight was in mankind.*

Afterwards, Wisdom set to work, building a house and laying a table, calling people to her feast. And so did the incarnate Word, calling people to follow him, and to eat and drink and live.

Pray for:
The United Reformed Church in the United Kingdom

In the presence of God

John 1.1-14

**For Word and Wisdom,
creating and shaping,
calling and refreshing,
all your people give you thanks.**

God, I thank you for making me who I am,
maybe not just as I would like,
but the person you chose me to be.

I thank you for making me to play and work
and, though sometimes I think the balance is not quite right,
you have given me both joy and creativity.

I thank you for making me to know there is right and wrong;
even if it could be easier to see the difference,
I know you want me to choose.

I thank you for making me unique,
sometimes, I think, a little strange,
but still of such great value.

I thank you for calling me to stay in your house,
an unlikely guest,
for whom a feast is spread.

I thank you for making me in your own image,
and, when that image was marred,
for restoring it by your Word.

I thank you for making me to live in your presence,
not that I am always aware of it,
but I know you are there.

**For Word and Wisdom,
creating and shaping,
calling and refreshing,
all your people give you thanks.**

Read: John 3.13-21

'This is the judgment: the light has come into the world, but people preferred darkness.'

These are words spoken to Nicodemus, who came to Jesus by night. So, did he come to the light or not? He came to Jesus, but he came in the night. He got it half right! That's me all over, and most of the people I know. We creep up to the light, half afraid at what will be revealed, half longing for its illumination.

All the world is caught in the trap, transfixed in the beam of God's judgment as it sweeps across the darkness, exposing petty jealousies and grand cruelties alike. People scatter and run, hiding in luxury or depravity, running from the dazzling, yet wishing they - we - could see. Or we think we can see, and become blind guides, which is worse.

Well, fine, now read verses 16-17 again. And, for good measure, Romans 7.21-25.

Shine

John 3.13-21

God of light,
you shine like a street lamp,
revealing the homeless man huddled at its base
and the woman hoping for business.
Your light shames us who look on
but makes their faces holy in its glare.

You shine like a Christmas light,
too gaudy and too early for some,
bringing innocent and vulgar pleasure to the city.
Your light shames the sophisticated
but brings delight to the children.

You shine like a sanctuary lamp,
a tiny hopeful holiness in the echoing dark,
a sign of a presence in our loneliness.
Your light shames the profane and ungodly
and brings sanctity to our world.

You shine in the twinkle of an eye,
a shining, soaring zest for life
that will not lie down with the demons of despair.
Your light shames the cynics
and brings abundant life to the poor of heart.

**God of light,
you shine in the world.
When we prefer the darkness
turn our faces to the light.
Teach us not to fear
but to welcome your shining presence.
God of light,
we turn to you.
Let us shine with your pure, clear light.**

Read: John 8.51-59

'In very truth, I tell you, before Abraham was, I AM.' They took up stones to throw at him.

This is another of the hidden 'I am' sayings. These are recognised as blasphemy by the non-believing Jews, and with awe by the disciples - the believing Jews (see John 6.20 and 18.16). This example is the most blatant, since, as well as claiming identity with the 'I am' of Exodus 3.14, Jesus clearly states his pre-existence, not before creation as in John 17.5, but before Abraham, and the beginning of God's relation with his people.

It certainly finishes the argument. Either he's mad and dangerous, or, which the untutored readily believed, he really was the long-awaited Messiah.

We live at a time which is longer *after* the coming of Jesus than Abraham's time was *before* his coming, so our perspective is different. After all, we believe that Jesus is still around, which is just as unlikely as Jesus' claim to have been around before Abraham. And we are, many of us, just as sophisticated as the learned Jews, so our intelligence may well revolt at the unlikely claim.

For us too, the stark reality of Jesus' claim cuts through the arguments: either 'I AM', or he's not.

Remembrance Sunday
Pray for: the British Legion 48 Pall Mall, London SW1Y 5JY, **the Peace Pledge Union** 6 Endsleigh Street,London WC1H 0DX **and the Fellowship of Reconciliation** 40 Harley Rd, London SE11 5AY

Before Abraham was   John 8.51-59

Eternal God,
before we were born,
you were there,
working in the womb,
letting life be.

Before we could speak for ourselves,
you were there,
leading us with love,
washing us with grace.

Before we could decide for ourselves,
you welcomed us to your knee
and took us to your heart.

When we had only just believed,
you had already forgiven us.
Before we could keep to the law,
you had pronounced us innocent
and called us just.

And then, when we went to war,
you had already won the battle for life.
When hope seemed lost and our security in danger,
we remembered our home with you.

Now we look forward to a new peace
and find again that you are there before us.
Before Abraham was, and before all time,
you are God, the great 'I am.'

**Eternal God, go before us,
and we will follow you.
You are our God,
and we will keep your word.
Be true to your promise -
may we never see death.**

Read: John 6.27-35

Jesus replied, 'This is the work that God requires: to believe in the one whom he has sent.'

No, no, Jesus tells them, you've got it all wrong. Moses wasn't the giver and the manna wasn't the bread from heaven. Working for the real bread from heaven is not doing, but believing. Believing is work, the work of God, and it earns the bread from heaven simply because the one whom God has sent *is* the bread from heaven.

The work will last our whole lives' long, and the bread will endure to eternity.

So
let's get to work
and enjoy the
feast!

Pray for:
The Congregational Christian Church in Ameican Samoa

Give us this bread!   John 6.27-35

Blessed are you, great God, for you bring forth bread from the earth.
Blessed are you, great God, for you have grown fruit from the vine.
Blessed are you, great God, for you have brought us to life.

In the beginning you watered the earth,
so that man and woman would have food and drink,
fresh bread to share each day
and new wine when the grapes are ripe.
You gave to our ancestors, Sarah and Abraham,
bread for their journey and wine for celebration.
You called Moses and the people out of slavery
and refreshed them with bread in the wilderness.
You gave Mary and Jesus daily bread
and, by a miracle, fed thousands who were hungry for your presence.
You gave strength to the first Christians,
as they shared bread and wine together
and praised you with happy hearts.
You have blessed many tables as, through the years,
your people have gathered.
Now, today, at the table of Jesus,
your offer us bread and wine for our journey,
bread for this our day and time,
wine to taste the pleasure of heaven.
As we eat bread today,
may the memory of your son Jesus
be alive among us.
As we drink wine the colour of blood,
may his death and rising to life
work their meaning within us.
Breathe the Spirit upon us
and upon this bread and wine,
that they may be heaven's food and drink for us.

Give us this bread, now and always.

Read: John 18.33-40

Jesus answered, 'King' is your word. My task is to bear witness for the truth. For this I came into the world, and all who are not deaf to the truth listen to my voice.'

The big question at the trial of Jesus was: what kind of threat did he pose? Was he some kind of royal claimant, who would undermine Roman authority by deposing their puppet king? Was he about to upset the delicate political balance which allowed the religious state to survive within a secular empire? People tried to fit him into their own patterns of authority and power, but he gently and persistently showed that there was another way.

The temptation is still there. The monarchic Jesus, in majesty, Lord of all the earth, is a strangely alluring figure. The hymns which sing his praises are exciting, and suggestive of positions of great power for those who hear his voice.

But let not the praises of King Jesus deafen us to his voice. His task is not to make us powerful, but to bear witness to the truth, and this is far less comfortable to hear, for his words challenge our aspirations. 'King' is still very much our word, not Jesus's.

Homelessness Sunday
Pray for: The Churches
National Housing Coalition
Central Buildings, Oldham Street, Manchester M1 1JT

Hosanna to the King!   John 18.33-40

Hosanna to the King of Kings!

who left his home
and walked along dirty tracks,
who spent his time with children,
preferred prostitutes to princes,
and was mocked in purple.

Hosanna to the King of Kings!

who washed feet,
was unafraid of leprosy,
gave away his rights,
and was enthroned on a cross.

Hosanna to the King of Kings!

who was rejected by religion and state,
levied no taxes,
would not be ashamed to be seen out with me,
and wore a crown made of sticks.

Hosanna to the King of Kings!

who can be found in prison,
or ill,
unclothed,
as a stranger,
needing bread.

Hosanna to the King of Kings!

who came to serve,
not to be served,
and shares with us his royal blood.

Read: John 7.25-31

'Certainly you know me,' he declared, 'and you know where I come from. Yet I have not come of my own accord; I was sent by one who is true, and him you do not know. I know him because I come from him and he it is who sent me.'

KNOWING

You may like to try this exercise in a group, or alone:

Think of a person who is well known to all the group – a public personality or someone from the same church or neighbourhood.

Let each member of the group add something about the person, so that a picture of him/her is built up. The additional details may be physical description (e.g. colour of hair), lifestyle (s/he likes chocolate, dislikes heights . . .) or some event in his/her life, (s/he climbed Mount Everest, spoke well at the Bible Study, called me a prune . . .)

Discuss how well the group knows the person in question. Who knows her/him best? Is there someone outside the group who knows the person better?

Now try the same exercise with God. Let each member of the group add some detail from scripture, or their own Christian experience. What does it mean to *know* God? Who in the group knows God best – or does that question no longer make sense? Is there someone outside the group who might know God better, and from whom closer knowledge of God might be sought?

This exercise, whether undertaken as a group or by an individual, might lead to a deep sense of God's presence, or to a negative sense of guilt and failure, if people feel that they do not know God as they ought. A group or individual should be prepared for either possibility, and give or seek pastoral care if needed.

World AIDS Day
Pray for: CARA (Care and Resources for People Affected by AIDS/ HIV) The Basement, 178 Lancaster Road, London W11 1QU

Looking for the one

John 7.25-31

Jesus our brother,
we are glad today
that men and women once looked into your face
and saw God.
We are glad that in your gentle look
we can find love for our longing and joy for our pain.
We are glad that in your face,
and in the faces of others,
we find those who know and love us.
We are glad and full of thankfulness
that, when hope seems small and tender,
we may look again into the faces around us and find strength.
Keep us glad, loving God,
and when we are faint-hearted and the night is chill,
smile warmly upon us once more that love may burn again.

A blessing:

Go in peace.
Look for the face of Christ
in all whom God sends to you.
And the blessing of God,
lover, beloved and friend of lovers,
be with you,
now and always. Amen.

Read: John 5.36-47

*'You study the scriptures diligently, supposing that in them you have
eternal life; their testimony points to me, yet you refuse to come to me
to receive eternal life . . . . Do not imagine that I shall be your accuser
at the Father's tribunal. Your accuser is Moses, the very Moses on
whom you have set your hope.'*

At a youth meeting in Te Atatu congregational church in New
Zealand, at which the gathering consisted mainly of Cook Islands
people, a discussion arose between the young people and their
elders. What would make the gospel come alive to young people?
They began from a discussion of outreach, but ended with the vital
question of Christian nurture within the church. Young people,
even brought up in a strong Christian tradition, need to hear the
gospel message in language which is relevant to their lives.

Much of the discussion was about tradition. When religious
tradition is closely allied to cultural identity, it may become
difficult to separate the two. It is tempting to study the scriptures
and find arguments to bolster what are really cultural norms.
The temptation is strengthened by imperialism - as in the early
missionary movements from Europe, and by the isolation of a
culture - when, for example, members of an ethnic group have
moved to another country.

Perhaps it is inevitable. After all, the Pharisees showed us the way.
Careful study of scripture will provide justification for anything
from fascism to egalitarianism, from total abstention to holy
orgies, and for a huge range of patterns of religious practice.
What fun! With real care, the teachings of Jesus can be almost
totally ignored.

And then Moses will rise up to judge us. For Moses and the
prophets pointed to the living God, and to Jesus, in whom alone
we, in all our variegation, find eternal life, and without whom,
lose it.

Bible Sunday
Pray for: The Congregational Union of New Zealand

When truth stumbles   John 5.36-47

Can you blame me, God,
for wanting scripture to be plain and reassuring?
I like my answers neat
and, with all those laws,
I'm sure there must be one for every case.
A Bible, half words of comfort
and half rule-book.

Sometimes I imagine I know you so well
that I've nothing more to discover.
But now I am not so sure.
There are bits of the Bible
which, if I'm honest,
I would rather ignore.
Some of it is violent, unjust -
stories of slavery
and cold-blooded revenge.
Worse still,
there are verses which ask more of me
than I would like to give
and tell me more of you
than I would like to know.

So I take the bits I like.
I suppose the trouble is,
I try to fit you to my own image
by making my own version of the Bible
from my favourite verses.
A scripture collage
with truth a casualty.

God, give me the courage
to listen to you.
I'll be ready to hear,
whatever you say.

Read: John 1.19-28

*'Then who are you?' they asked, 'We must give an answer to those who
sent us. What account do you give of yourself?'*

This is a deputation of priests and Levites sent specifically to find
out who this troublesome preacher is. And they ask in very specific
terms. Are you the Messiah? No. Elijah? No. The Prophet, then?
No. But there has to be an answer. John has to fit into the scheme
laid down by the Hebrew Scriptures.

John picks up on a prophetic passage, seeing himself as the
forerunner, not just of the Messiah, but of God's coming: *I am a
voice crying in the wilderness, 'Make straight the way for the Lord.'*
(Isaiah 40.3)

Isaiah was looking forward to the release of God's people from
their long exile in Babylon, and their return to be reunited with
their compatriots left to moulder in a much reduced Jerusalem.
The great highway would be the place for a second Exodus, across
which would come, not the people of God, but God himself,
returning to the Land of Promise, and the City of Zion. The picture
is wider and richer than the simple matter of where one individual
fits into the scheme.

It was not long before the disciples, and others, were asking Jesus,
'Who are you?' As with John, the answer was more complicated
than their narrow categories would permit. Yes, the Messiah, the
Son of the Living God, but also the fulfilment of that mysterious
Hebrew figure, the Son of Man; yes, the long-awaited King
descended from the house of David, but also the suffering servant,
showing a new way of living.

John the fore-runner and Jesus the long-awaited are both more
than theological ideas, categories, neat fulfilments of specific texts.
John bursts from the pages of the New Testament as a crazy,
fanatical, tragic figure, whose courageous message led the way
to the transformation of the world.

Pray for: The Presbyterian Church of India

A voice in the wilderness   John 1.19-28

God, how good it is to raise our voices
and to welcome your presence among us,
a stream in the desert, a rose in the wilderness!

Make straight the way for the Lord!

From our slumbers we rise to praise you.
All that demeans and belittles us we shrug off,
as we stand strong and confident before you.

Make straight the way for the Lord!

From all we do to keep you from us,
from all the evil that is in us,
from the gloom that would overwhelm us
and from all that would harm us,
set us free!

Make straight the way for the Lord!

We share our hope together,
that you will come to us as prophets tell,
bringing peace and justice to a tired and twisted world.

Make straight the way for the Lord!

God, come to us in Jesus and save us!
Let the waste places of the world be made new again!
Let the wicked be routed and the righteous shout with joy!

Make straight the way for the Lord!

Read: Luke 1.57-66

. . . his mother spoke up. 'No!' she said, 'He is to be called John'

Poor, blessed Elizabeth. For so long barren, so well on in years, and
now giving birth to a child conceived by her husband who came
home struck dumb, but suddenly fertile.

How strong this woman must have been; strong to bear her shame
through the years during which they were unable to conceive a
child; strong as the wife of a priest who spent time in the close
presence of the God they shared; strong to withstand the rigours
of pregnancy and childbirth in her later years.

No wonder she could name her child in the face of natural family
bewilderment and opposition.

> 'You'll call him Zechariah after his father . . . .'
> > 'But there's never been a John in your family . . . .'

Like Mary, she had to bear the strange mission of her child, and his
imprisonment and shameful death – if indeed she was still alive by
the time Salome demanded his head for her mother.

Poor Elizabeth – Elizabeth blessed and strong!

Pray for: The Churches of Christ in Malawi

Blessed and strong   Luke 1.57-66

Living God, how strong you make us!

We are children
but you let us lead the way.
We are barren
but you make us fertile.
We are brushed aside
but you give us central place.

Living God, how strong you make us!

We are counted as nothing
but you see our value.
Our homes are taken from us
but you want to stay with us.
We have no job
but you have a purpose for us.

Living God, how strong you make us!

Our children are taken from us
but you give us a new family.
Our enemies come to destroy us
but you win the victory.
Escapism and addiction threaten us
but you give us freedom.

Living God, how strong you make us!

We thought we were lost
but you found us.
We looked for an answer in violence
but you showed us an innocent child.
We needed a messiah
and you came for us.

Living God, how strong you make us!

Read: Matthew 2.1-12

entering the house, they saw the child with Mary his mother and bowed low in homage to him; they opened their treasure chests and presented gifts to him: gold and frankincense and myrrh.

This is almost the year's end. Christmas presents have been given and received. The approach of the new year is traditionally a time for reflection, and for new resolutions.

Traditions cluster around this time of year. Another is that the three gifts represent three elements of the life of Jesus - gold for a king, incense for a priest, and myrrh presaging his death.

> You may like to consider what manner of gifts you have brought to Jesus in the last year, not to please him, but to honour him, to celebrate his royal priesthood and remember his saving death. Consider, too, what will be your gifts in the coming year?

Pray for: the children in your own family and church

Love's look

Here, today,
we stand and stare.
We look at your beauty and holiness,
as wise men once gazed upon an innocent and unknowing child.
And we are filled with gratitude and praise
that this wonderful thing has happened among us -
God, you are with us.

Here, today,
we stand and stare.
We look at ourselves
and we look at the world we have made.
We gaze on our own beauty and holiness,
for you have made us so like you
and you have placed us
in a world full of splendour and liveliness.

Here, today,
we stand and stare
at the evil and the terror and the sadness
and we pray it could be otherwise,
in ourselves and in all around us.
We are sorry that there is ugliness and profanity.
We repent of our own failings ...
We confess that our world is marked by danger and distress.

Here, today,
when the worldly wise may kneel before innocence,
we ask for your forgiveness
and a new beginning.

Loving God, by your grace,
give us again that beauty and holiness
that is our true nature.
Look on us with love's renewing gaze.

INDEXES:

1. TITLES OF PRAYERS

INDEXES:

2. BIBLE PASSAGES

INDEXES:

3. SUBJECTS FOR PRAYER

CARA (Care and Resources for People Affected by AIDS/HIV)	*1 December*
CCBI (Council of Churches for Britain and Ireland)	*7 January*
CCOM (Churches Commission on Mission)	*22 September*
CCRJ (Churches Commission on Racial Justice)	*8 September*
children	*29 December*
Christian Aid	*19 May*
Christians in Public Life	*11 August*
Church Computer Users Group	*28 April*
Churches National Housing Coalition	*24 November*
Churches Together in England	*28 January*
CSSA: (Christian Survivors of Sexual Abuse)	*25 August*
CWM Women's Advisory Group	*17 March*
CYTUN (Churches Together in Wales)	*21 January*
Fellowship of Reconciliation	*10 November*
Free Church Federal Council	*4 February*
local church	*7 April*
local churches	*4 April*
local ecumenical groups	*5 April*
Peace Pledge Union	*10 November*
SCIAF (Scottish Catholic International Aid Fund)	*19 May*
SCM Press Trust	*5 May*
South Africa Council of Churches	*16 June*
World Development Movement	*20 October*

Special Sundays/Days

Bible Sunday	*8 December*
Christian Aid week	*19 May*
Education Sunday	*4 February*
Homelessness Sunday	*24 November*
Martin Luther King Day (15th January)	*14 January*
Mothering Sunday	*17 March*
One World Week	*20 October*
Racial Justice Sunday	*8 September*
Remembrance Sunday	*10 November*
Soweto Day	*16 June*
Unemployment Sunday	*25 February*
Week of Prayer for Christian Unity	*21 January*
World AIDS Day	*1 December*

MOUNTAINS OF DOUBTING (7.7.7.6.4.5.)

John Maynard (1925-85)

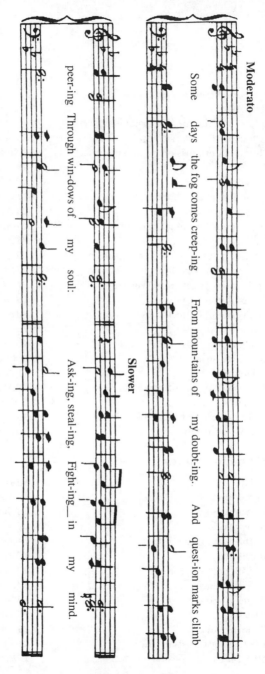

Moderato

Some days the fog comes creep-ing From moun-tains of my doubt-ing. And quest-ion marks climb

Slower

peer-ing Through win-dows of my soul: Ask-ing, steal-ing, Fight-ing—in my mind.

Words by Cecily Taylor (1930-)
Music Reproduced b y permission of Stainer & Bell Ltd. and Women in Theology from 'Reflecting Praise'

VERSE 1: Here is a ta-ble that is round, that is round. And strong are its num-bers wide its bound-ries. Better ar-tist-ry can-not be found not be found. And we are that ta-ble that is round.